TALL TALES

By the same author:

Stories
UNDER TWO SKIES
SOME PERSONS UNKNOWN
THE AMATEUR CRACKSMAN
THE BLACK MASK
A THIEF IN THE NIGHT
STINGAREE
WITCHINGHILL
THE CRIME DOCTOR
OLD OFFENDERS AND A FEW OLD SCORES *

Novels
A BRIDE ROM THE BUSH
TINY LUTTRELL
THE BOSS OF TAROOMBA
THE UNBIDDEN GUEST
THE ROGUE'S MARCH
MY LORD DUKE
YOUNG BLOOD
DEAD MEN TELL NO TALES
THE BELLE OF TOORAK
PECCAVI
THE SHADOW OF THE ROPE
AT LARGE
NO HERO
DENNIS DENT
MR JUSTICE RAFFLES
THE CAMERA FIEND
FATHERS OF MEN
THE THUSANDTH WOMAN
HIS BROTHER'S BLOOD *
THE GRAVEN IMAGE *

•   *published posthumously*

Tall Tales
and short'uns

E.W. Hornung

Compiled and introduced by Peter Rowland

Nekta Publications

(2015)

To Alan John, tracker-down of unconsidered trifles,
without whose unstinting and indefatigable assistance
this volume could never have been produced, and
with many thanks to Scott Gaunt for the cover design.

.

CONTENTS

Introduction

By the latest reckoning, E.W. Hornung wrote fifty-five short stories between the summer of 1887 and the end of 1900. Nearly all of them were published and re-published in magazines or newspapers in English-speaking countries throughout the world. Thirty-two (including eight which chronicled the rise and fall of A.J. Raffles) subsequently featured in books. After discounting three which, at the very outset of his career, were written primarily for boys, we are left with twenty which have been virtually forgotten since the end of the nineteenth century — and two, indeed, which have never been previously published *anywhere*. Twelve of those stories appear in the present compilation, including the two newly-transcribed items. (The manuscripts of the latter, 'A Dog and his Day' and 'Cabin-Companions', are housed in the Cadbury Research Library of the University of Birmingham, catalogued as items MS 127/A/2/1/3 and 4 respectively: I am extremely grateful to the Library for granting me access to them and to Bernard Hornung, on behalf of the Hornung family, for sanctioning their publication.)

Information about the sources of these stories will be found at the end of this book. It can be safely contended that the quality throughout is reasonably high and soars at times to levels which can only be described as masterly, for the author speedily acquired the art of spinning a yarn and holding his reader's attention from the opening paragraph to the last. Allowance needs to be made, however, for the melodramatic nature of the opening story, 'The Stroke of Five'. Written by Ernest W. Hornung (as he billed himself) when the author was only twenty-one, it seems to have been the very first tale he penned that was intended specifically for adults rather than children. Its inclusion, after momentary editorial hesitation, is justified primarily because this was, in retrospect, a noteworthy event. (The opening sentences are also autobiographical, although the author — perhaps fearful of being dismissed as little more than a juvenile scribbler flexing his puny muscles — saw fit to add a year to his age.) Thereafter, however, it is possible to track the development of his skills and quiet subtlety, both in drama and humour and the maintenance of unfailing tension, in an approximate chronological sequence. It should also be acknowledged at the outset that many of these tales are set in Australia — primarily in the Riverina area of New South Wales, where for health reasons Hornung had lived and worked for a period of two years in the mid-1880s. He never returned to Australia after the age of twenty but, in one sense, he never left it, for this was a country which had fired the exuberance of his imagination in a manner which the British Isles rarely succeeded in doing. (After 1900 the preponderance of Australia in his fiction substantially diminished, but four short stories written in 1917, partly for therapeutic reasons, would take him back there, in spirit, for one last visit.)

Hornung's imagination was that of a poet — as many of the descriptive passages in his stories and novels make abundantly clear. It is appropriate, therefore, to take advantage of the present occasion to include (in the batting order) a short but very relevant poem, 'The Stockman's Cheque', and to wind up the proceedings with his chronicle of an epic encounter between two village cricket teams — the Whizzingham stalwarts and the doughty warriors of Hurry-cum-Up. At which point, having superintended a preliminary handshake between the author and his potential readers, the editorial umpire must fade dexterously into the background…well, *almost* at any rate.

Peter Rowland
Wanstead, London

2

The Stroke of Five

I am a clerk employed in a large mercantile house in Lombard Street, and am in my twenty-third year. I live with my parents and other members of my family in an outlying suburb ten miles from the City, whither I journey by train every morning, returning in the evening. In the office I have gained a character for quiet, plodding industry. At home, I maintain my character for quiet, and am in addition considered a dreamy book-worm and unsociable into the bargain. I am of medium height, slightly built, and, it must be confessed, the reverse of muscular. I could never discover that I possessed other than commonplace features; and the same verdict, perhaps less qualified, would probably be given by others. Thus much about myself it is necessary to state before I attempt to relate that which befell me on the morning of March 24, 1886.

On the evening of March 23, I had been for the first time to see the Lyceum *Faust*. If I am a lover of books to unsociability, I also carry love of the drama to extravagance; at least, so I used constantly to be told in the family circle a year ago, for I go to the play less frequently now. I was, in fact, an inveterate 'pitite', and seldom a week went by, especially during the season, without my visiting one of the West End theatres.

As early as six o'clock on the afternoon of the 23rd, I had taken up my position outside the pit entrance at the Lyceum, with the result of a seat in the front row.

The performance enthralled me. Being no linguist I had read no more than a translation of the work of Goethe, and I was therefore untroubled by doubts as to the textual rendering of the original. For three hours I lived in the land of Romance.

I sympathised with the actors in the tragedy. With senses and nerves strung to the highest pitch of sympathy I concentrated my whole attention on what passed before me. And yet I very soon felt that sympathy becoming absorbed in the evil genius of the play! Gradually the influence grew upon me, until Mephistopheles exercised over me a greater, an immeasurably greater charm than any other personage in the play.

My heart warmed to this scarlet prince of darkness! His plausibility played upon my fancy in the beginning, his ingenuity fanned my fancy into admiration, his unfathomable cunning turned admiration to holy reverence! The supreme badness of the fiend won me over to the wrong side in spite of myself. The influence of the fiend intoxicated me. Each poisoned arrow of subtle sarcasm struck acute enjoyment into my soul. All through the play, when the fiend was on the stage, my eyes saw no other form, my ears heard no other voice. But on the Brocken, I absolutely revelled in the majesty of the fiend!

No thought of the actor influenced me. For the time I thought only of *this* demon as *the* demon. The power of imagination was very strong within me.

As I walked from the theatre to the station I could not repress a momentary feeling of shame and wonder that my sympathies had been so completely given to the wrong side. Who but myself had ever witnessed *Faust*, and enjoyed the play from this standpoint? Who but myself had gazed at the picture from the reverse side, and delighted in it?

The thought was fleeting, and the unanswered questions did not vex me. My mind quickly returned to its demon-worship.

As we reached Flower Bank, my suburb, the hands of the station clock pointed to a quarter to one. I walked down the platform, through the little gate at the level crossing, and on the

4

accustomed way home. I had noticed no other passenger quit the train at Flower Bank.

In walking from the station to my father's house I usually followed a narrow footpath that runs between the boundary fence of the railway and the boardings at the backs of the gardens of a road of Queen Anne houses parallel to the line. After a quarter of a mile these houses end, though the path continues, and my way lay diagonally across a field, which brought me opposite to the turning into our own road.

I had proceeded about a hundred yards from the station along this path. My mind still dwelt among the weird scenes of the evening. I was crossing a wooden bridge spanning a ditch that interrupts the footway. All at once I became sensible of a gliding footstep behind me.

The right forearm of a stranger was thrust beneath my left arm, and a strong hand grasped the muscle of my arm.

I started terribly, and looked sharply round. The night was very dark, but I could make out that the man was tall and thin, and somewhat inclined to a stoop. A long close-fitting cloak enveloped him from neck to heel. He wore on his head a large sombrero that effectually concealed his features.

The stranger continued to move onward, and in spite of my intense surprise I could not choose but move onward too. For half a minute neither of us uttered a syllable. Then my companion bent his head until it was near mine, and in a deep, solemn, not unmusical voice, spoke.

"You must allow me to accompany you," he said. I stammered, faltering, that his company would afford me pleasure, if our ways were identical. I was filled with fear which I tried hard to suppress, and it was with difficulty I succeeded in keeping my limbs from trembling violently.

He took no notice of my words, but glided forward with silent steps, his hand still grasping my arm. How like was this tall, lithe, bending figure; this deep, penetrating voice, to the form and voice of the weird image present in my mind! My imagination, already stimulated and overwrought, was ripe to surmise the supernatural. Was I dreaming, or had the prince of fiends come himself to seek me out because of my ungodly fascination?

My companion spoke again:

"You have been present at *Faust*." The tone had in it no note of interrogative inflection. It seemed to state with authority known, undeniable fact.

"Yes," I managed to murmur, after a short pause of speechless surprise. How could he know where I had been?

"And did you admire — Mephistopheles?"

I started painfully. Whence came this strange dark man to probe the inmost thought of my brain? What was he — man or devil?

The tone was one of grim banter, and reminded me of the caustic utterances of the Evil One, that I had gloried in during the evening.

"He was grand — magnificent!" I said with enthusiasm, in spite of my fears — in spite of my wonder.

"Ha, ha! A clever performance — a fair imitation; but not counterfeit — no, no; not counterfeit! Wait until you see the real Satan! Ha, ha, ha!" He hissed the last words into my ear, and the laugh that followed them was hoarse and blood-curdling.

I fairly shook with terror. My knees knocked together as I walked. I felt the perspiration gather on my brow.

Thank God! here was the field. At the other side of this field was the first lamp-post of my own road — the first light I had seen since leaving the station! How the jet flickered its invitation to safety, its welcome that awaited me! Now I would bid good night to my dark companion, and run home: run home, as fast as my legs could carry me — run! run! run!

I gathered courage from the distant friendly light, and said:

"My way lies across this field. If you still continue by the path, I am afraid I must leave you."

For the first time my companion arrested his gliding walk, and stood still in the pathway. He regarded me for a moment; then said slowly:

"Leave me? Leave *me?* Boy, you little know to whom you speak! No. You cannot leave me. You shall not leave me. Shall not — neither now nor evermore!" The words were hissed rather than spoken, with hoarse, vibrating distinctness. The strong hand closed round the puny muscle of my arm. Madman? Yes, or devil! I felt it worse than useless to resist, and yet —

"Help!" It was a short sharp cry that burst involuntarily from my lips; not resolute enough to summon aid.

My companion's left hand was thrust with lightning rapidity into his bosom, and with the same movement the gleaming blade of a knife protruded through the right breast of his cloak, and pressed against my side.

"One other sound like that, and I leave you with *this* in your heart! Now let us go on."

On again together. My heart was as if turned to lead in my body; but the very intensity of my fear gave me coolness and resolution. I would humour him, I would agree with him, I would stay with him; — for this there was no choice, but I would stay with simulated willingness. An attempt to escape, or the faintest cry, would now, I knew, mean death. We skirted the field in silence, and were once more between boarding on our left and the Railway Company's fence and quickset hedge on our right. This path, as I knew, ended in a frequented road a quarter of a mile ahead.

7

The knife had disappeared, but the left hand of my companion was still buried in his bosom. There was a silence of some three or four minutes, broken only by the sound of my companion's measured gliding footsteps and my nervous tread.

At last he broke silence with one more solemn, low, precise articulation.

"You came by the last train?"

"I did."

"At what time does the first morning train pass here?"

"Five o'clock, I think."

"You *think*! Come, boy, be sure."

"Five o'clock."

"Good. In that case we shall spend exactly four hours together, for it is now one o'clock."

Now one o'clock! Only one! That meant only a quarter of an hour had passed since I left my train. Impossible! It could not be. An hour — two hours — must have gone by since then. And must I spend four more hours with him? Sixteen times as long as I had been in his company already, if this man spoke truth regarding the time? Absurd! But this man did not speak truth; this man —

A distant church clock chimed the hour, and then struck — one!

Something must be wrong with the church clock. Three was the hour it was meant to strike, not one. But what did this man mean when he said "We shall spend exactly four hours together"? Could he mean that he would leave me then, and escape from the district by the early workmen's train? If he did, I would have the police on his track before the sun was fairly above the horizon! He should be locked up this very morning — locked up for a dangerous — that was if he were not a — Oh, how the cold bony hand clutched my arm!

We were drawing near the road. Through the darkness of the night I could just distinguish the shadowy forms of houses sparsely built: but no lights in the windows. No lights to encourage me — and warn my companion. I fancied I could hear the measured tread of the policeman on duty.

The railway on our right now ran through a deep cutting. The path we followed led inwards from the edge of the embankment. A hundred paces on, an old disused bridge arched over the line, which from the station to this point was singularly straight. Beyond the disused bridge a curve commenced, and a furlong from the first bridge a second bridge, newly built, spanned the line, the curve still continuing. Where the path turned inwards from the railway a tall untrimmed hedge rose a few paces from the railway fence. The hedge took the place of the fence as right-hand enclosure of the path, and between hedge and fence there was entrance to a wedge-shaped grassy slope, which stretched to the foot of the masonry of the bridge. I had strolled down this slope in daylight, and knew that near the bridge, where the earth had once been dug away, the slope changed into a steep descent to the level of the lines; though immediately next the fence the descent remained gradual.

As we approached the entrance to the slope between hedge and fence, I bore somewhat to the left of the path, hoping my companion would notice no break to the right. In my over-anxiety to keep to the path I must have palpably pushed against my companion, for his right hand clasping still more tightly my arm, and his left diving once more beneath his cloak -

"Fool!" he hoarsely muttered. "So you still desire to tread again the paths of man? We shall see to that ere long. Meanwhile come *my* way."

Resistance was madness; but, as I yielded, the last ray of hope of deliverance went out in my heart. Abandoning myself to I knew not what, I suffered myself to be led from the path of comparative safety and probably succour. In the power of this monster, bent on Heaven knew what, I might as well be in the heart of an African jungle as in in the lonely hollow at the base of this old bridge. A terrible calm came over me, like that which I had read of experienced by men in the clutches of some wild beast. Surely here was no distant analogy!

As we descended the grassy slope, and my companion chose as if by instinct the easy downwards path into the hollow, the deep sepulchral voice that had uttered few words during the latter part of our walk spoke in a louder tone than before, but still with the same clear, penetrating emphasis.

"The pit before us is opportune. Come, get you down, young man. Here we shall have no interruption, and I have much to say to you — before five o'clock!"

We stood in what indeed was little short of a pit. Behind us, and to the right, a grassy wall of earth twenty feet high; to the left the moss-covered masonry of the old bridge; in front the railing that divided us from the line, on the level of which we now stood.

"Yes, we are safe from interruption here," continued my tormentor. "Now do as I bid you, and, remember, at the smallest deviation from my command your life is forfeited — before its time! You see that star overhead?" pointing upwards, "it is the North Star. Fix your eyes on the North Star, and do not remove them until I tell you."

I bowed assent, for fear clogged my tongue; and, raising my head, I made a desperate effort to look clearly at the star.

He continued speaking.

"You visited the theatre known as the Lyceum last evening. You sat at the left-hand end of the first row in the pit. I sat within a few yards of you, in the last box on the lowest tier."

I kept my eyes fixed steadily on the star. Some effort was necessary, to enable me to sustain the terrible tension of my nerves; and this effort of gazing fixedly at the North Star, and knowing that on this action of gazing my life depended, was a relief to my whirling senses. But I started as I gazed upwards. I dimly remembered having seen once or twice between acts a solitary, dark, gloomy face in the box nearest to me; which, whenever I had noticed it, seemed to be regarding me earnestly. So wrapt up had I been in the play, that, though I now remembered the searching scrutiny of my face by the dark eyes to the left, at the time I had been practically unconscious of it.

"Yes. I watched you from the box farthest from the stage, in the lowest tier of boxes on the left side of the house. I have occupied that box many nights, very many nights," he sighed wearily; "but," he added with deep, tremulous, terrible emphasis, "I have sat there, night after night, *in disguise*: yes, in human, earthly disguise!"

His voice rose, and gathered more awful, vibrating intensity with every word. I gazed upwards still, but the star danced before my vision like phosphorus in a vessel's wake.

"In the guise of a man have I sat there! In the garb of a mortal!" he almost shrieked. Then, his voice lowering to deep, quivering, unearthly tones, "Cast down your eyes, O child of man, and know me for what I am!"

I threw up my arms and staggered backward. What was this I saw before me?

A dark haggard face, shining with a pale green light. Arched eyebrows, hooked nose, gleaming teeth. The tall bending body clothed in a black flowing robe. A dark skull-cap on the head. Two long arms stretched towards me, the bony hands and fingers shining with the same green light that

11

illuminated the face. Thin green smoke ascending from face and hands!

What was this — vision or reality? Where was I — in dreamland or in — Hell?

The grinning lips moved:

I am — the Devil!"

I neither breathed nor stirred. The grinning lips moved again.

"Know now with whom you are dealing: with the King of Darkness — the Evil One — Satan — the Devil — call me what you will!"

My breath came in stertorous respirations. I placed my hand on my brow: my brow was cold and clammy. I moved my foot: the damp grass was beneath it. I looked upward: the pale cold stars smiled mockingly upon me.

No — I was not dreaming.

All at once I heard a hurried footstep on the narrow path above. It must be some belated wayfarer, some mortal who would help me. I opened my mouth, but the tongue clave to the palate. Before I could articulate, a flaming hand and gleaming blade were upon my breast, and a flaming face a foot from mine!

I fainted....

When I recovered my senses, the Satanic form was bending over me.

"Come, come! I give you no further grace to conquer this folly. If you cannot be calm now, you die without further fuss. If you choose to live a little longer, stand up, attend, and be sensible. Now, which is it to be?"

With a stupendous effort I managed to rise to my feet and stagger to the wall of the bridge, one strong bony hand grasping my limp arm. I leaned against the masonry, and obtained relief from contact with the dank moss-covered stones.

"You elect to live — a little longer?"

I nodded feebly.

"I thought so. I studied your face and head pretty closely with eye and glass during the evening. Your face is commonplace enough, but it is a wonderfully clear mirror of your mind. Your mental homage to — my imitator was, for instance, plainly written on your face. Then I studied your head, for, you see, you wear your hair closely cut. You are tenacious of life, and concentrativeness is very strongly developed. Is it not so?"

Damp shining fingers passed carefully over the central surface at the back of my head.

"Just as I thought. Now in combativeness," feeling behind the ear, "you are deficient. That, too, I found out through my glass. Ha, ha! an immortal has to keep abreast of the sciences of man, my friend; I studied phrenology once, in the guise of a student."

If there was comparison in my feelings just then, I was glad when the cold fingers were removed from my head.

"So you appreciated Mephistopheles — the sham Mephistopheles, eh? Well, I grant you it is a fine performance, a wonder mimicry — for a man! I have sat, in my guise of mortal, and watched this mimicry of myself many nights, very many nights. It has pleased my fancy, it has flattered me — with the sincerest flattery. I have over and over again watched carefully the players; and over and over again, still more carefully, the spectators. And until this night, young man, no mortal has witnessed those scenes and, in his heart, thrown in his lot with Mephistopheles. You never took your eyes off this mock Satan; and as you gazed, I read in your face admiration,

13

awe, and even reverence; anon exultation and gloating, then again only admiration."

A reader of thoughts! but could I wonder at that in —

"And since you fell so deeply in love with the sham demon, I, the real demon, determined — ha, ha! — to reveal myself to you!"

Surely the night must be waning now! The pale blue stars had changed their positions since my enforced contemplation of the only stationary body among them. And if the night was waning, daylight must ensue. And surely daylight would dissipate this fiend — or phantom! Or should I wake — no! I was awake already. Oh God, that I could think all this a dream! But if not a dream, what was it? what — ?

"Mortal, it is time to tell you why I followed you, and sought you out alone. Can you guess?"

I shook my head.

"I brought you alone to a lonely place for the forming of a contract the like of which you saw made in the early part of that play. You are to sell your will to me!"

His voice, calm and dispassionate for some time past, returned to that hissing horrible emphasis which had characterised his earlier utterances.

"You are to sell your will to me! But do not think of reward, like the reward of youth that the spurious spirit held out to his victim. I offer no reward — but eternity with me! Give me your hands, and look in my eyes!"

I placed my limp numbed hands within the cold bony hands held out to me. The dark face, less lurid now, but shining still, came close to my face. Dark fiery eyes transfixed my eyes.

We stood thus, motionless, for I know not how many minutes. Then without movement or flicker of the steady gaze, the hands were withdrawn from mine, and gently waved to and fro before my face. Then back to their grasp of my hands.

14

"Do you surrender your will to my will?"

I no more than heard the words. Some mental cord seemed to have snapped. I heard and saw distinctly, but I did not connect what I heard and saw with thought. Instinctively I repeated:

"I surrender my will to your will!"

A long pause. Then with subdued triumph my companion spoke:

"You are in my power — mind and soul and body — in the power of him you call the Evil One!"

The deep voice sounded metallic and far away. I felt no longer an actor in this grim scene by the old railway bridge, but a beholder — even as I had been a beholder of the Brocken's hideous orgy. I could now converse dispassionately and mechanically, for I felt that the power of speech had returned. But the power of intelligent thought had gone, and with it all sensation of fear.

My companion's eyes never relinquished their steady gaze into mine. He spoke again:

"How far advanced is the night?"

"It is almost four o'clock," I said, peering closely at my watch.

"Four. In another hour the first streak of dawn will show in the east. And in another hour — at five, I think you said — the first morning train passes this place."

"The train is due at Flower Bank three minutes past five."

"Come then; let us move from here, and stand upon the metals."

No wonder at this proposition, no curiosity concerning motive disturbed the calm of the stupor into which my senses had merged. My hands still on in the grasp of my companion, his eyes still on mine, I was pushed gently to the fence. The

15

fence was low here, and the hedge broken. I stepped over with little difficulty, and *he* followed.

Once more I leant against solid stone. It was the inner wall of the arch. Our hands and eyes were still joined; the former in firm, clammy grasp; the latter in mutual unflinching state of horrible intensity on the one side, and apathetic stupor on the other.

We stood in silence. The distant church clock, the sound of whose chimes had reached us from time to time, chimed the quarter after the hour.

"What was that?" The questioning voice sounded as far away as the chimes.

"A quarter-past four."

"Then we have three-quarters of an hour more of this."

"Is that all?" I asked languidly.

"At five this ends."

"Do we part then?"

"For a time."

"And where do I go then?"

"To *Hell*."

The words, the hoarse tone, did not disturb me. I felt only dimly puzzled.

"How do you mean?"

"At five you die."

"At five I die!" I repeated dreamily. "How?"

"By suicide."

Suicide! What was that? I used to know — but now — no; I could *not* think.

"Tell me," I said wearily, "How? I do not understand."

"By laying your body across these metals. The early train will do the rest."

"Ah!"

16

Ding — dong — dell — ding — dong. Half-past four from the distant church spire.

A pause. Eyes and hands unaltered. At last:

"What of you?" I asked.

"I look on."

"But you will be seen!"

"No."

"No! How is that?"

"Because I am invisible."

A pause of minutes.

"I am invisible to all mortals on this earth — save you. To you I have revealed myself — before taking you to my realm for ever."

Ding — dong — dell — ding — dong: ding — dong — dell.

A quarter to five. The figure opposite seemed more distinct in form and outline. Yet sunrise would not be for more than an hour.

"Yes. Sunrise is not until six o'clock. And you will never see the sunrise."

That my thought was read occasioned me no surprise. I merely repeated dreamily:

"And I shall never see the sunrise!"

"Never! Ha, ha, ha!" A fiendish laugh. "This morning you breakfast with Pluto. With Pluto? No, no. With me! With Satan in his own realm!"

The deep sepulchral tones once more:

"Now lay yourself across this line of rails, your shoulders resting on that far band of steel, your feet pointing at me — so. And fold your arms across your breast — so. And keep your eyes steadily fixed upon my eyes. That is well. Now, if you move limb or muscle, this steel blade of mine must do the work instead of the steel wheel of the engine. But the engine will be better and quicker. Hark! I hear it! The train has left the next station."

Langford station is one mile and a quarter from Flower Bank station; therefore three-quarters of a mile from where I lay.

He — in the long cloak and skull-cap, stood by the side of the line, a yard from my feet. His expression was one of fiendish exultation, but the pale green light on hands and face seemed to have vanished in the grey light of earliest dawn. He went on speaking:

"Hark! The sound grows more distinct. You must not move your eyes from mine, for if you break — hark! the hour is striking! how punctual they are here!"

Ding — dong — dell — ding — dong: ding — dong — dell: ding — ding — ding — dong — . Ding. Ding. Ding. Ding. Ding.

As the last stroke of the distant clock died on the air, and the noise of rushing wheels grew louder and louder, I closed my eyes to shut out the horrible form in front of me. I turned my face to the right, and reopened my eyes. Within thirty yards of me was the hissing, snorting locomotive. I saw the engine, I heard the shriek of the whistle, and — I came to my senses!

I came to my senses, but awoke from no dream. The same second I saw the engine the mesmeric spell that had bound me was broken; that same second I knew my position; and that same second I redoubled my legs and body over my head, and executed the one gymnastic feat of my life!

As my body rolled into the six-foot-way a demon yell burst from the other side of the rails. I saw between earth and air a figure in a flowing robe, with outstretched arms and naked knife, in the act of springing upon me! ...

When I recovered consciousness this time, I found myself in the porters' room at Flower Bank station. My head, pillowed

18

upon rough corduroy, was supported between the knees of a porter. Before opening my eyes, my ear caught some of the conversation going on around me.

"'E's bin and well nigh done for this poor young gen'leman," said one voice.

"But was done for himself, poor *lunatic*! They're bringing him this way on a hand-truck," said another.

"Hollo, Bill, what did you find about the pore man? Anything as'll tell us who he is?"

"A brass-ticketed hotel-room key, a purse full of sovereigns, a packet of phosphorus, and six programmes of the theatre! No clue to his name, or where he come from ...."

It was some days before I knew that my companion of that terrible night was a gentleman who had been out of his mind for years, his mania being that he was the Devil! He had escaped a week before from the custody of his friends, taken rooms, without causing suspicion, at the Grosvenor Hotel, and spent every evening in witnessing Mr Irving's "wonderful mimicry" of himself! On every other point he had been not only sane but intelligent.

The Cooeying Woman: an Australian legend

Razorback is a wild and rugged mountain on the southern edge of the Farewell Ranges, in Victoria. Its sides are so steep and rough, its surface is so broken, and the growth that covers it so wild and undisturbed, that from the green plains to the south the mountain barrier looks formidable indeed. To the north, behind Razorback, Rose Town settlement nestles among the Rangers. On the south side, at the base, stands the ruins of a hut built in the early days of the colony. A rough track, gradually ascending round the western spurs of the mountain from the hut to Rose Town, may still be traced. But the rugged, upturned face of Razorback shows neither track, nor fence, nor landmark to this day.

It is many years since the rude skeleton at the foot of Razorback was a habitable hut. It was put up by the first owner of the broad acres below the mountain, and was occupied by the shepherd of his outlying flocks. In 1854 the shepherd was William Bell, and with him in the hut lived his wife Maggie.

The Bells had married in Bonnie Yorkshire only to seek their fortunes together in the new land of gold. Labour in those days was very dear throughout the colony, and soon a considerable balance was credited to William Bell in his master's books. But high wages could not reconcile the Bells to Australia. When summer parched the pastures, and all beneath the dark-blue sky was sere and sombre, they longed for the green lanes of Yorkshire, and the yellow rippling fields of corn, to cool their scorched eyes. What cared they for dark-blue skies, and gorgeous birds that knew never a note of song?

And where was the charm of fantastic flowers that gave no scent, compared with their own wild country roses of old?

"O, Will!" Maggie used often to say, "let us go home, lad! We have enough money now — let's take ship while we have it."

"Wait a bit, my lass — a little longer," he would answer, with tenderest love in his voice. So months went by, and Christmas found William Bell still shepherding flocks at the foot of Razorback, and Maggie still working and waiting.

"Come, a pannikin of tea, Mag," cried William Bell, heartily, as he entered the hut after penning the sheep for the night, "for I've a journey to go."

"A journey, Will? O, where?"

"Where but to the township, this Christmas Eve! — to do a bit of shopping."

"Will, don't you go to Rose Town tonight," implored the wife

."And why not, my lass? Why, I'll be back before daylight."

"But it's five miles by the road, Will."

"But I don't go by the road. No, no. It's over the mountains for Will. And, bless you, I know every inch of old Razorback," he added, catching a look of fear on his wife's face.

"They say it is dangerous" she whispered.

"Dangerous!" said Will, "why, who knows that mountain as well as I, who am hunting strayed sheep on it every week of my life? No, lass, 'tisn't dangerous — for me. And — you mustn't be foolish, but just look out for what I'm going to bring you from the township."

Bell ate his meal with a cheerful air, kissed his wife tenderly, and taking a stout stick, left the hut and started up the mountain side.

She did not gaze after him. She did not watch out him of sight from the hut door. But she sat gazing at the glowing embers in the fireplace — thinking. Her thoughts must have been sad ones, for presently great tears gathered in her eyes and fell heavily in her lap.

Tears from heaven, too! noisy raindrops falling upon the iron roof. She went to the door; all was dark and lowering. Surely the leaden sky is very close to the earth; surely, too, it is touching the top of Razorback. But what is yon blood-red streak in the sheet of lead — seen for a moment, then gone? And what means this horrible cannonade overhead, that makes the ground quiver and the timbers of the hut rattle?

A storm — a summer storm! Short-lived, yet of terrible violence! And her Will out in it, out on the top of Razorback! More lightning; more thunder; then a fierce whirlwind from the south, and driving rain. Again thunder, and more blood-red gashes in the leaden darkening sky. She fell hysterically upon the rude bed, and covered her head with the blankets, to shut out sight and sound. There she lay, trembling, sobbing, praying, until a dizziness came over her brain and consciousness left her.

When Maggie Bell awoke there was no sounds of rain on the roof. She rose and looked out of the door. The sky was clear and star-lit.

What time was it? She could not tell, but it must want a long while to dawn; and Will could not be back before dawn. But no more sleep for her tonight. She would set to work and tidy the hut against Will's return — no more than her share towards making their Christmas day a bright one.

While she was busy, the dawn burst over an eastern range. She went on with her work until it was finished, and then lit a fire and set about preparing their breakfast, for Will was overdue now.

The water in the "billy" upon the fire bubbled over but no tea was added, for Will did not come.

The sun climbed high is his bed of blue, but no cheery "cooey" from the mountain side announced the husband's return, and when Maggie looked out no human creature met her anxious gaze.

A sickening fear gradually stole over the heart of the girl. Memory of the storm, and the blinding rain, and the lightning, and the knowledge of the rough, intricate wilderness that covered the mountain, came together to torture her. When the sun was at its highest, and still no sound nor sign of her husband, Maggie took her straw bonnet and started off at a fast walk along the rough track to Rose Town.

When she reached the township, she went straight to the general store, then to the blacksmith's forge. These were the principal buildings at the settlement, and at each the answer to her enquiries was the same, shattering her brave hope that her husband had been detained in the township.

William Bell had never reached Rose Town.

She walked back to the store. "You must raise a search party," she said; "my husband is out on Razorback. He may be hurt, or lost. For God's sake, help me to find him." Then she walked quickly and quietly through the township, and struck straight into the thick bush that covered the side of Razorback. She was not seen during the afternoon by the other searchers, and did not return to the township. But most of the party had heard from time to time a strange shrill cry, like the penetrating "cooey" of the blacks, but that the long note was so high and shrill, and the terminal wail so mournful. It must be Maggie, they said, cooeying for her husband.

For days afterwards the search was continued, without success. Nor was anything seen of Maggie Bell. But the sad, sustained cooey was heard from time to time by the searchers.

23

One dark night, a strange, wild female figure stole into the township. The woman begged some bread at the inn, but on being curiously regarded, fled with a wild cry in the direction of Razorback. The people said it was Maggie Bell, gone mad, and that she would roam Razorback until she died.

A new shepherd was installed in the Bells' hut, and he alone saw Maggie afterwards — "Cooeying Maggie", as folks now called her. She would come down the mountain side at intervals of a few days, and put one simple question to the shepherd: "Is he come back yet?" Then, reading in the shepherd's face her answer, she would turn with a sob back to the mountain; but not before than man had thrust upon her bread and meat, and, perhaps, covering.

Once a strange drover, who was camping at the foot of the mountain, was startled by hearing a shrill, unearthly cooey, close, as it seemed, to his tent. The dogs ran into the camp cowering with terror; and the camp was immediately struck and removed by the terrified drover.

Cooeying Maggie, the fire of madness in her dark eyes, and her dark hair hanging in tangles about her ragged bodice, tramped for many weeks the cruel face of Razorback. Often she would pause, place her hand to her poor lips, and utter the shrill weird cry that was borne so far, yet never brought answer. Never answer, save the chattering of parrots, the chirrup of locusts and cricket, the hoarse mocking laugh of the jackass.

The brain of Maggie Bell had long ago given way, and, little by little, the body followed. The ground she traversed became daily less, and each cooey fainter and shorter than the last. Once the shepherd tried to detain her, seeing here altered looks, but, with a fierce cry, she burst from his kindly touch, and he never saw her more. Soon the cooeying on the mountain ceased.

There are those who still say they hear the wild, weird, despairing cry, mingled with the wind that blows over the mountain; and these believe that Razorback is haunted by the spirit of the cooeying woman.

Cabin-Companions

A few years ago I was appointed chief mate to the *Lake of Killarney*, of the celebrated 'Lake' line of Australian Clipper Packets, owned by Messrs. Burgiss and Maclaren, of London and Glasgow. The advertisements stated that the *Lake of Killarney* was a "splendid iron sailing ship, of 1,819 tons register, 100 A.1 at Lloyds", made mention of "excellent accommodation for all classes of passengers"; and specially intimated that "an experienced surgeon accompanied the ship". And in these recommendations I am bound to say there was very little exaggeration. The ship was well found, well manned, well commanded; and I have seen her do her fourteen knots without knowing it. The few passengers carried were comfortably berthed, and so well attended to that the undertone of grumbling was less audible than on most voyages. As to the doctor, he was at least a distinctly able man — which can be said for but a few of the raw medical students and partially-qualified surgeons who are daily advertised by the shipping agents as "experienced".

Our advertised time for sailing from Greenock was 3.00p.m. on Saturday, 1 March; and by that hour all the passengers were aboard. By four the tender had steamed away with the passengers' friends, with cheers and the waving of tear-stained handkerchiefs. But we were not destined to weigh anchor that evening. Indeed, for thirty-six hours we lay at anchor in the self-same position, owing to a foul wind and reported heavy weather in the Clyde; and it was not until two o'clock on the Monday morning that our tug ventured to tow us from the Tail of the Bank. Even then, after a few hours at sea, stress of weather drove us back into Rothsay Bay for two more days.

26

And when at last we parted with the tug, we had to boat down channel against head winds and a heavy cross sea. On 6 March we were off St John's Point; on the 7th we passed Lambay Island; and on the 8th, or a full week after nominally sailing, we finally left behind us Tuskar Rock — the Start Point of the Irish Channel.

The *Lake of Killarney* was not designed to carry a number of first-class passengers; the saloon accommodation was as limited as it was well-appointed; and there was nothing remarkable about the half-dozen occupants of the state-room. But Dr Kestevson, whose cabin was on the starboard side of the after deck-house, struck me at once as being no ordinary man. He was about thirty years of age; tall, well-built, and handsome, with classically cut features and fair curling hair. He showed himself from the first to be genial, sympathetic, and shrewd; and it was understood that he had temporarily abandoned a lucrative practice in search of a few months' rest and ozone.

In the doctor's cabin, contrary to custom, a fellow-passenger was berthed: a Mr Middleton, who had taken his passage at the last moment, when all the state-room berths were engaged. This man was also, in his way, as handsome and as noticeable as the doctor, and of much the same age. He was also black-bearded and bronzed, and had already spent ten years in Australia, whither he was returning after a brief trip to the "old country".

When at last we beat clear of the Irish Channel our troubles were by no means over; indeed, they seemed only to have begun. For eight mortal days we beat against hard winds just outside the Bay of Biscay. Though close-hauled under snug canvas, I do not think we sailed our proper course for a single hour during the whole time. So surely as eight bells sounded through the ship, "hands 'bout ship" was passed for'ard. Then round she went on the other tack — only to add another acute angle to our zig-zag course four hours later. There was plenty of discomfort for the ship's company: we officers kept double watches; while for'ard, the seas at one time ran so high that they leapt over the fo'c'sle as we plunged forward, and fell in a cascade on the main deck, the fo'c'sle within presenting a miserable picture of mist and damp and dripping oilskins. A heavy miscellaneous cargo, such as the Clyde floats out so prolifically, laid us low in the water, and we made very dirty weather of it indeed.

As for the passengers, I think they must have had a bad time of it — but the stewards know best. Now and then they would struggle up in couples for an hour or so, but they always seemed glad to totter below again: and the cuddy table was almost entirely deserted at meals. I pitied their abject misery: my heart would have bled for them, only that a few voyages in the passenger trade so brutalize a man in some things! Two landsmen, however, were to be seen on deck day after day through it all. When the doctor was not attending his patients, or busy with pestels and mortar in his cabin, he might be seen briskly pacing the weather side of the poop arm-in-arm with Mr Middleton. The captain and I soon became friendly with the pair. Their appetites were as hearty as ours, and their enjoyment of life under adverse winds a good deal keener. They soon got their "sea-legs", too, and became as sea-footed as we were. The ship never went about without Kestevson and Middleton lending willing hands at the braces. A strong mutual friendship appeared to have been quickly established between them.

Foul winds do not blow for ever: the case in point suggests several opposite saws, but I prefer to confine myself to a plain statement of facts gathered from the old log-book which is by my side as I write: to whose unvarnished record, even more

28

than to memory, I trust while penning my plain statement of the events of that voyage. On 16 March, then, we ran 130 knots on our course; on the following three days, though the wind felt light, what wind there was was favourable; on the 23rd, in latitude 29°. 25'.N., we fell in with the North-East trades; and then at last came really "plain sailing". And it may here be observed that the accomplishment of the remainder of the voyage was as swift as the outset had been tedious.

The luck had changed at last; and the *Lake of Killarney* plucked up her spirits and battled along merrily into the seas of eternal summer. Then we decked her in her summer suit of sails, and on she sped freer than ever. Now the decks were crowded with passengers, reading, playing draughts, and amusing themselves in countless indolent ways beneath the awning. A concert was got up by the doctor and one or two others; and a capital entertainment it was too. Kelverston was the vocal star of the evening. He sang a couple of good songs really well, and was vociferously cheered by the crew, with whom he was already a great favourite.

"Upon my word, doctor," said I one evening as I stood at the brink of the poop, during the first dog-watch. "I have seen friendships struck up abroad ship before, but I never yet sailed with a pair of chums half so thick as you and Mr Middleton." The latter, who had been pacing the poop by the doctor's side, had just gone below, and his friend was evidently awaiting his return.

"He is the best fellow I ever knew," said Kestevson with enthusiasm. Then he added with a laugh: "You are right, Mr Kelly; we certainly *are* as thick as thieves; Damon and Pythias were fools to us!"

"Yet he seems to be a quiet sort of fellow," I said. "He never seems to have very much to say. I for one can get precious little out of him."

"Wait until you know him better," returned the doctor. "He is naturally reserved. He and I have been thrown together from the beginning."

"What is he?" I asked.

"He has been out in the Colonies for many years, principally in the bank. He has seen all the Australian cities, and is a most interesting man about his travels. Ah, here he comes." And the pair resumed their evening constitutional.

I have mentioned that Kestevson and Middleton shared a cabin on the starboard side of the after deck-house. My cabin was the fellow to theirs, on the port side, the compartment being divided by a thin partition only. Many a night when I turned in until the morning watch the talking of the friends kept me awake longer than was pleasant; but I never had the heart to rap through to them a request for silence. By raising myself in my bunk and laying my ear to the bulkhead I could have overheard every word of their conversation, had I been so minded. But though, with my head on the pillow, I could catch no more than the intonation of the voices, one thing struck me night after night as peculiar: the conversation was carried on almost entirely by one voice — the doctor's. Monosyllables and occasional brief sentences were Middleton's share of the dialogue. But then, in spite of the doctor's opinion of him as expressed to me, Middleton was without doubt a queer, reserved fellow. I had almost added silent, but his silence was not consistent. At times he was the most silent man in the ship; at others no spirits ran higher than his. When in the latter mood he was boisterous, witty, good-tempered — in a word, capital company; when in the former, his looks were gloomy, fierce, forbidding, and he would speak to nobody — always excepting the doctor, with whom he appeared glad to enter into conversation at any time. His temper, however, knew no medium: it was either mercurial or else it was morose.

Therefore it struck me as strange that all the times the sound of the friends' voices reached me in my cabin, Kestevson was never once the listener, the commentator; that the conversation was never once carried on with anything approaching a fair exchange of words.

Somehow or other, as I found myself liking the doctor better each succeeding day, so I gradually grew to dislike and distrust Middleton. What was the meaning of his alternate fits of gaiety and surliness? — of his unvarying urbanity to the doctor, whatever his own mood? Why should a man, who barely made himself agreeable to other folk, save spasmodically, and to my thinking with visible effort — why should such a man be at pains to worm himself into the close friendship of a man like Kestevson? Could such a friendship, on Middleton's side, be disinterested? Was not Middleton taking all he could get and giving nothing in return? These were some of the questions which puzzled me, and which often kept me awake after my neighbours had ceased talking.

One sultry night (it was thirty-six hours after we had crossed the Line, therefore 5 April) I lay awake longer than usual tossing on my hot bunk, and filled with uneasy thoughts as my ear caught the rise and fall of the doctor's voice punctuated by Middleton's monosyllable. At length the voices grew fainter and fainter; until in their stead I heard only the languid lick of the waves as we slid slowly through the water. Then that sound also died away, and no other filled my ears in its place. All was still as the grave. Presently my eyes assumed the activity that was denied my ears. Sharp and distinct a vision rose before them, and this is what I saw — The doctor's cabin: Kestevson lying asleep, his powerful arms sprawled over the single sheet that covered him; his head thrown back and its fair waving hair falling over the pillow: from above, a dark face glaring down on the sleeper — an arm and hand descending with a gleaming blade — the blade coming closer and closer to the white throat of the sleeper — ! —

A low laugh close to my ear brought me to my senses. Had I been dreaming? To this day I cannot answer that question satisfactorily! The laugh at any rate belonged to no dream. It was repeated: a long, low, grating sound, pregnant with malice and triumph.

I could not stand this, coming as it did on the top of my vision. I slipped from my bunk and out of the cabin, and was quickly outside the doctor's berth. The door was wide open, and hooked back from the outside; a curtain fell across the inside of the doorway; a dim light was burning within. I drew the curtain an inch aside and peered in. Shall I be believed when I tell of the sight which met my gaze? There lay Kestevson in the lower bunk, precisely as I had seen him a minute before in my dream! From the upper bunk leant Middleton, with his head bent so that I could not see his face, but only a mass of black, wiry hair. The only points in which what I actually saw from my realisation of a minute ago was there: I was unable to see Middleton's face; and the murderous knife held so close to the sleeper's throat was now, I saw, merely a harmless ivory paper-knife.

I remained with my feet glued to the deck and my eyes riveted on the two men until Middleton slowly drew himself up and laid down the paper-knife. As he did so I had time to note that his face was deadly pale, and that his hand shook as he straightened the swinging candle. Then I heard him fling himself back on his pillow with something between a deep sigh and a groan.

I crept noiselessly back to my cabin, devoutly hoping that I had been unobserved by the second mate and the midshipman of the watch. There was no further rest for me that night. My vision and its strange realisation was inscrutable, inexplicable.

I was terribly mystified; and not only suspicion but intense alarm were awakened within me. Eight bells struck while I was still completely bewildered; and I turned out to the muster of the watches sick at heart and full of foreboding.

Next night I lay on my bunk, sleepless and attentive to every sound, from eight bells at midnight until eight bells at 4.00am, when my watch on deck began. But I heard nothing. The night after that, however, I both heard and saw sufficient to compensate for twenty barren vigils; sufficient not only to increase my suspicion of Middleton, but to envelop Kestevson also in a haze of mystery.

During the day the wind had freshened considerably. Since crossing the Line we had been fanned by merely the fringe of the South-East trade winds; today for the first time we had felt their full breath. When I left the deck at ten we were slipping beautifully through the water at nearly ten knots an hour, keeled slightly over on the starboard tack with every foot of canvas drawing. I had not long to wait before the companions entered their cabin. They were talking, and for a wonder Middleton was bearing his share in the conversation: unless I was mistaken, they were arguing together. I blew out my candle and sat up with my ear close against the bulkhead. When suspicions are awakened, I take it that eavesdropping is no crime against honour. For a minute I could not distinguish what they said; but afterwards the words came quite distinctly to my ears.

"I tell you," said the doctor in his eager, ardent tone, "the spirit is a mean one, a contemptible spirit. I say it is inadmissable to the mind of the rational man — but let me hear your story."

"When we have turned in I will tell it you. Meanwhile — whatsoever you may say about it — there are cases in which I think that some spirit is praiseworthy — noble, even."

33

"Not unless evil can be undone or the laws of God and man satisfied. Merely to cry quits in the sum of mutual injury is worthy only of the lower animals," said the doctor.

"A fair sentiment!" sneered the other; "but I doubt, my good fellow, whether you yourself would be inclined to practise what you preach so glibly. As for me, it is my habit to pay off old scores and to be even with any man who does me a mischief. I make no secret of it; I take no credit for it; I think myself neither better nor worse for it; — but I will be even with all men, Kestevson, so long as I live."

"Then all I can say is that in my opinion, Middleton, the statement is ignoble and its principles rotten."

Middleton laughed. "You are inconsistent," he said. "You who defend — as I have heard you defend — dishonesty and cowardice on the plea that circumstances alter the whole scale of blame — you of all people start pitching into honest vengeance! But now, since you're comfortably tucked up and at my mercy, I'll tell you — "

"Ay, do. Who is the laudable Nemesis?"

"A man I knew in Australia."

"And his victim — that is to be?"

"One of your brotherhood — a clever saw-bones. Does that prejudice you?"

"No: go on."

"Well, my friend came home with me last spring. He had been out there three years; his only living relative in England was his father, with whom he had parted on bad terms; he was going home to see his father once again at the old fellow's earnest request. His father was a country doctor. A year before my friend started for England he heard that the old man had taken into partnership a young fellow newly-qualified. Now, when we landed, what sort of news should you think

34

greeted my friend — the returned Colonist — the prodigal come home for his governor's blessing?"

There was a pause. I suppose Kestevson signified by a gesture his inability to guess what was coming; for I presently heard Middleton go on coolly, though with greater earnestness than one usually throws into an impersonal anecdote:

"Why, the blackguardly junior partner had murdered the old man — that was all! You start; but it wasn't the kind of murder to make you or any other nervous person start. (And you do seem nervous tonight, Kestevson. How is it?) There was no steel or lead or strychnine in the case: those approved means were a good deal too honest and not sufficiently cold-blooded for our friend the junior partner. How was it done, then? Oh, a slow but sure, simple course. First, a management of all accounts by the obliging junior; next, systematic embezzlement — What's wrong, Kestevson?"

"Nothing. I only said - how terrible!"

"But you really look pale, Kestevson; — shall I open the door and let in more fresh air? No? — very well, then, I'll go on. — Systematic embezzlement, I was saying: that resulted in difficulties; which resulted in bankruptcy — and suicide of senior partner. That was all. There was nothing to prove against the junior partner — he had cooked the accounts too cleverly for that; and the dead man did not leave behind so much as an incriminating letter, worse luck! After the inquest, our friend simply packed his portmanteaux and cleared out. Of course hard things were said about him, and to his face; but bless you! His hide was too thick to mind *that*. But my friend — "

"What about him?" put in the doctor quickly.

"He solemnly swore to avenge his old governor. By wonderful luck he got on the scoundrelly doctor's track. He is on his track now! — he has even got his man in view!" said

35

Middleton in a deep voice. "And there will be an instance for you of what I call just revenge when the quarry is run to earth," he added with a harsh chuckle.

There was another pause, during which I could hear only my own heart's beating as I pressed my ear close to the bulkhead. Then someone put a question in a strange voice which I should never have recognised as Kestevson's had I not known there could be no third person in their cabin: — "What was the name of — the junior partner?"

"I must not tell you: he is a member of your profession, and a contemporary of yours. Maybe you were at the same hospital together — *maybe he is your most intimate friend!*"

"The name of the senior partner, then?"

"Was Philip Maynes," replied Middleton hoarsely.

I could remain where I was no longer. A drama was being played in the next cabin — I must be eye-witness of it as well as ear-witness. In a couple of seconds I stood outside the door of the doctor's cabin. The door was closed, owing, doubtless, to the cooler weather; but the port-hole was open, and through it I stealthily peered.

For the second time I saw Doctor Kestevson lying on his back in the lower bunk — but what a contrast to the former night! One arm was tossed on the pillow behind his head, the fingers twitching nervously; with the other hand he grasped the blankets at his side in a bunch. His fair hair was in disorder. His face was white as death, the teeth tightly clenched, the eyes fixed on the opposite bulkhead in a wild stare: the smooth broad forehead glistened in the candle-light with beads of perspiration — again, like death! Never have I read on face of man so plain a signature of abject fear! Middleton sat on a chest with his back to me, leaning forward towards the doctor: I could not see his face: he did not speak. Kestevson's broad breast rose and fell violently; but neither did he speak.

36

How long did that silence last, I wonder? Four double-strokes on the ship's bell rang out from the fo'c'sle, proclaiming that it was four o'clock in the morning. I had to hurry to my cabin, hastily throw on my clothes, and be at the break of the poop to call over the names of my watch as the men gathered aft. As I wrenched myself from the spot the last I saw of the doctor and his companion showed their positions unaltered and the same wild expression of fear on the face of Kestevson. Confound the midshipman who stuck eight-bells! I could have reprimanded him for his punctuality!

I saw little of Middleton and less of Kestevson that day. The doctor was strangely unsociable for him. He avoided us all; he particularly avoided Middleton, I thought. When they were together I could see that it was because Middleton had forced his company upon the doctor. Middleton, for his part, seemed less moody and erratic than usual: he had gained in good humour what Kestevson had lost. I don't know whether anyone else noticed the changes — probably not; but I had my perception terribly quickened, and nothing escaped my observation. I saw, in spite of Middleton's altered manner, a dark magnificent cloud cross his face as he chatted affably with his chum: sometimes the cloud deepened into an ugly frown, sometimes it ended in a sardonic smile. I saw, too, that the doctor's face and lips were colourless; that his eyes were lacklustre yet painfully alert; that his movements were restless and convulsive.

That night no sound reached me from the next cabin. But at two bells in the morning watch (5.00a.m.), as I stood by the wheel looking up at the sails, a white figure stepped up to the poop, and began pacing rapidly to and fro.

"Now doctor," I said, moving over to the figure and discovering it was Kestevson, "can't you sleep? It's cool weather for pyjamas on deck — we will soon be out of the tropics, you know."

"No," he answered wearily; "I cannot sleep."

"What is it, prickly heat?" I asked with a laugh.

"I am hot," he said; "but it is not prickly heat."

I placed my hand on his forehead: it was burning hot to the touch. If the man was not in a raging fever, then his brain must be on fire!

"Man alive!" I cried; "get below! You will catch your death up here in those pyjamas, in that state of heat! Get below, and turn in."

He gave me a queer, bewildered look; then without a word he went.

On 12 April we passed out of the tropics. On the 16th we began to "run down our easting" — in other words, to sail from west to east longitude. Between then and our crossing the meridian of Greenwich, eight days later, I had little time to observe the mysterious pair. During those days we made excellent running, but unsettled weather and frequent squalls caused her ladyship to require the nicest attention. Sometimes we were obliged to take in the royals twice daily; once or twice we even furled t'gall' sails. You may be sure, however, that when I was able to do so I kept a keen eye on Middleton and Kestevson. What I saw confirmed my first impression as to the reversal in the mutual relations of the two men. So far as appeared, the friendship was as firm as ever; the difference was that Middleton was now the active and Kestevson the passive party. So much, indeed, were the two together, that at times I half thought that my doubts and fears and suspicions were as unfounded as my eavesdropping had been unwarrantable. And this feeling, I think, kept me from sharing those doubts, suspicions, and fears with the skipper. Moreover, though I continued to lay awake during my watch below of nights, it was no longer because of talking in the next cabin: I heard no more conversations in that quarter.

On Tuesday the 29th, when about six hundred miles south of the Cape of Good Hope, we fell in with a gale of great violence, which blew until the Thursday night. On the Monday the barometer plainly indicated that dirty weather might be expected. On Tuesday the atmospheric depression had increased; the sky was leaden and restless, and the sea ran turbulently. At noon the first squall struck the ship. Fortunately the wind came from W.S.W., so that we were able to run our course before the gale under upper-topsails; had it been a head wind we should have been obliged either to heave-to or to close-haul under the strongest canvas. At three in the afternoon we were scudding along at less than fifteen knots an hour. I have seldom seen the sea run higher, even off the Cape. The tops of the great rollers broke from time to time over our weather-rail, flooding the main deck until the water gradually found an outlet through the lee scuppers. But that was nothing to the veritable "green seas" which poured inboard in tons more than once during that night and the following morning, when the storm was at its height. When we shipped a green sea, the waist of the vessel was for a short space of time completely under water. The smooth green mass leapt over our weather bulwarks and crossed the deck in dense volumes as the vessel keeled, when a part of the mess cleared the lee rail with a second leap and part dashed against the lee bulwarks with a roar and an upheaval of foam and spray. Passengers were warned not to venture amidships, and indeed, between main-mast and fore-mast neither seaman nor landsman could willingly have lingered. When morning broke, the watch stood at the entrance to the fo'c'sle, and the officers on the poop; all hands were encased in oilskins and sou'westers; two men only proclaimed themselves landsmen by their ulsters and cloth helmets — Middleton and the doctor held on side by side to the weather-rail of the poop.

About breakfast-time one of the cuddy stewards slipped and fell on the wet deck near the galley, hurting his knee, and was assisted into the steward's cabin in the for'ard deck-house. Kestevson, who saw the accident, immediately hurried forward.

"Look out, doctor!" I sang out from the break of the poop; "we'll have a sea over in a minute — look out you aren't soused!"

"All right," he sang back, hurrying along the starboard side.

"Look out!" I roared again.

It was too late! I had seen the smooth green mass riding up under our weather bow, and — as I shouted my second warning — the monster reached its full height, rose above our starboard bulwarks amidships, and toppled down on our deck in tons! Kestevson was in the act of skirting the main hatch; he had hold of nothing; the immense volume of water caught him with its full force, instantly knocking him off his legs. For a moment we saw nothing in the boiling, seething sea that filled the waist of the ship. Then the vessel keeled over to leeward, and violently borne with the shifting mass of water we saw a dark object.

"It is the doctor!" cried some of the passengers. "Heaven help him! — he will be washed over the side!"

As they spoke, Kestevson's body was lifted by the rush of water to leeward — lifted clean over the trail! Had anyone rushed forward at that moment the same fate must have befallen him also. And it all took place in a moment! Those on deck who were not momentarily spellbound shrieked aloud in their agony of mind.

"Good God — he is gone!" "He's over!" "The doctor's lost!" "NO! — not yet! — look there!"

A pair of white hands were grasping the main shrouds just above the rail. The white face of the doctor could just be seen above the rail as the vessel rolled and laboured. Then there was a rush like a wild beast's along the deck — someone leapt up to the bulwark, twisting an arm and leg through the shrouds — one tremendous effort, and the doctor lay on the deck, stunned and bruised, but saved! Great Heavens! To think it had all happened in a single minute!

And now the worst of the water had discharged itself through the scuppers; and the pair were coming slowly aft, Kestevson dripping, pale, and blood-stained — Middleton only slightly flushed; and the people on deck were cheering like maniacs, for the favourite, the best-loved of ninety souls, had been pulled from the jaws of death by his dearest friend! To me, the white set face of the rescued man showed apathy and despair rather than gratitude; and the flush on the rescuer's dark cheek seemed to be a flush of devilish exultation. But the passengers yelled and cheered, and I heard one telling the other that the love of those two men passed the love of brothers; that either would go through fire and water for the other; that if one had perished, the other would have perished with him!

And now it remains for me to record the closing scene of the tragedy of that voyage.

On the evening of 9 May the ship was doing nine knots before a fresh W.N.W. breeze. The night was fine, and the sea running smoothly for those latitudes: our position at noon that day read, "Latitude 44°. 485, Longitude 76°. 46.E." I closed my cabin door shortly after nine o'clock, and was in the act of undressing, when the cry that makes the oldest sailor tremble rang through the ship — "Man overboard!"

"Man overboard! Man overboard!" was caught and echoed by a dozen voices; and as I dashed from my cabin another cry was added to the first — "The doctor! The doctor!"

The captain was issuing the necessary orders to put the helm to starboard, brace up the head-guards on the port tack, and clear away the starboard life-boat.

As I sprang upon the poop the passengers were hurrying up in mad excitement. The first thing I saw in the darkness and confusion was the figure of Middleton rushing wildly aloft.

"Stop him — stop him!" I shouted; but I was a moment too late. Without a word or cry Middleton sprang upon the taffrail and dived into the darkness and the ocean!

I ran back to the captain, crying: "There's another passenger overboard! Two madmen are in the sea! We cannot save them!"

"We will try," was the grim answer. "She's fast coming to; take charge of the boat, Mr Kelly, and call for a crew of volunteers."

Three times as many men as I required stepped forward. I made my selection, and in a minute we all stood ready at the gangway. In ten minutes from the alarm the way was off the vessel, and we were lowered away into the darkness.

A mile astern a small bright light shone on the expanse of swelling ocean, through the clear crisp air: it was the burning fuse of the illuminating life-buoy which had been thrown overboard at the first alarm. I steered for the light as the misin gave way with a will.

Nearer — nearer — and nearer still we came to the floating light. When a fathom from the light, the sound of a voice reached us across the water.

"They've hold o' the buoy — hurray!" shouted the men.

"Easy boys," I said, trembling with excitement. "Morrisey, stand ready in the bows, and you too, Denleigh; ship oars the pair of you."

"Aye aye, sir."

"We had come up to them; they were within our reach. With one arm Middleton clung to the buoy, with the other he was supporting the doctor, who appeared insensible. But, even as the men in the bows were reaching forwards, Kestevson's eyes opened — the yell of a madman rang over the sea — a pair of arms were flung wildly about Middleton's neck, and locked in Kestevson's deadly embrace he sank never to rise again!

"The doctor was mad, my lads." I said in a hollow voice. And when we had lingered about the spot for half-an-hour we rowed back to the ship.

I told the skipper all I knew. When we got home again, we made private but thorough investigations into the doctor's past history — particularly into that part of it which immediately preceded his joining the *Lake of Killarney*. And of that I have nothing to say, for I have told how Philip Mayne the younger, *alias* Middleton, recounted that part of Kestevson's history to Kestevson himself. But of Maynes's movements in England we could find out very little; and it is tolerably certain that none of us will ever know how long he had been on Kestevson's track; when he came up with Kestevson; whether he booked his passage in the *Lake of Killarney* by premeditation or on the spur of the moment; or what scheme of vengeance he had in view. That the story I heard him tell to Kestevson was the true story of Kestevson's ruining old Maynes, leading to the latter's suicide, was proved beyond the shadow of a doubt. From enquiries prosecuted in the Colonies, we learnt that young Maynes had borne the character of being wild, reckless, and passionate; but that he was reported a man of unvarnished honour and indomitable will.

The affair never became public property; all that the newspapers got hold of was that Dr Kestevson, of he ship *Lake of Killarney*, had fallen overboard by means unknown; that he had been drowned, and along with him one John Middleton, a passenger, in gallantly attempting to save Dr Kestevson's life. Before the end of the voyage I heard a steerage passenger saying to his companion: "Didn't I tell you — that morning Middleton saved the doctor's life — that they were like brothers? — that if one went the other would go too? My words have come true. Ah, William, there's been the hand of fate in this — or the hand of God!" So jealously did the captain and I keep to ourselves what we knew!

The Stockman's Cheque

There's a hut in Riverina where a solitary hand
May weaken on himself and all that's his;
There's a pub in Riverina where they keep a smashing brand
Of every sort of liquor short o' fizz.
And I've been an' blued another fifty-pounder at the pub —
You're very sorry for me, I'll be bound!
But when a man is fit up free with hut, an' horse, an' grub,
What the blazes does he want with fifty pound?

Why the devil should he hoard his fifty quid?
Who would be a bit the better if he did?
Though they slithered in a week,
When I couldn't see or speak,
Do you think I'm here to squeak?
Lord forbid.

The boss was in the homestead when he gave me good advice.
I took my oath, but took his cheque as well.
And to me the moonlit shanty looked a pocket paradise,
Though the boss had just been calling it a hell.
Then the shanty-keeper's daughter, she's an educated lass,
And she bangs the new pianner all for me;
And the shanty-keeper's wife, she sticks me up as bold
                              as brass,
An' the shanty-keeper's wife is good to see,

Two petticoats between 'em whisk you far!
But the shanty-keeper smoked behind the bar.
Oh, his words were grave and few,
And he never looked at you,
But he just uncorked a new Gallion jar.

We fed and then we started in the bar at nine o'clock;
At twelve we made a move into the cool;
The shanty-keeper he was just as steady as a rock,
And me as paralytic as a fool.
I remember the veranda like a sinkin' vessel's deck,
And a brace of moons suspended in the sky ….
And nothing more till waking and inquiring for my cheque,
And the oath of all them three I'd drunk it dry!

So that was all I got for fifty notes!
The three of 'em stood lying in their throats:
There was one that must have seen
I'd have beat him blue an' green
If I hadn't gone an' been
Off my oats.

Thank the Lord I'm back at last – though back wrecked and
                                        whisky-logged!
Yet the gates have not come open that I shut,
And I've seen no broken fences, and I've found no weak sheep
bogged,
An' my little cat is purring in the hut.
There's tea, too, for the billy-can, there's water in the tanks,
The ration-bags hang heavy all around;

An' my good old bunk an' blanket beat the bare veranda planks
Of the shanty where I blued my fifty pound!

Here I stick until I'm worth fifty more,
When I'll take another cheque from the store;
And with Riverina men
All the betting is that then
I shall knock it down again
As before.

Long Jake's Trip Home

Long Jake had been indulging in his periodical spree. The fact first dawned upon him with the dawning day, when a heavy driving shower beat him into the veranda and soaked him where he lay like a log. As the day advanced, the truth grew gradually sharper and clearer, and piece by piece he began to patch together those fragments of the past few days which still lingered, with blurred outline, in his memory. Yet, though his head ached again — perhaps from the mental effort, perhaps from other exciting causes — of the greater part of the time he was able to recall absolutely nothing. It was on Friday he had ridden into the township from his hut beyond Razorback, and, as a matter of course, parted with that thirty pound cheque to John Byrne, the publican: he was quite sure of that. It was now Tuesday afternoon, and John Byrne, the publican, had plainly intimated that the end of the spirituous tether which that cheque had secured was arrived at: alas! he was equally sure of this. But the interim was a nebulous void. Thus the knowledge that he had been four days drunk stole slowly into the blunted sense of Long Jake, as day steals into some cave deep in the mountains, forcing its laboured way through gap, rift, and crevice. But it was not until it came to catching and saddling his mare, with infinite difficulty and feeble vexation of spirit, that he fully realised and appreciated all that had gone on.

At last, however, he was in the saddle, sitting tight with thigh and knee, the upper part of him huddled into a ball. Not much of a man to look at, at any time: no grace of feature or of form: not even a really good seat in the saddle. Nothing of any account from head to heel. A small fresh-coloured face; crooked beard, turning gray; legs absurdly long in proportion to the rest of him, and that the shape of a bow. They called him Long Jake; for his ill-apportioned length was the man's sole individuality; and as for surname, it was never dreamed that he had one, either in this little township of King Parrot Flat or in the surrounding ranges.

"Well?" shouted John Byrne from the veranda that fronted his grog-shanty, as Jake rode round from the yard. "So you're off, eh? And when shall we see you again? Not for another six months, I s'pose. — So long." John Byrne spoke sadly, yet with the consoling certainty with which one augurs the return of summer while watching the falling leaves. For Long Jake was one of his regular sources of income — had been for years. To look at John Byrne as he stood there in his red shirt and cabbage-tree hat, tall and handsome as he was, you would never have taken him for a shark and a robber. On the contrary — though these terms, I assure you, would have been none too hard for him — you would probably have discovered in him a type of rugged, solid, honest manhood. At all events everybody else did — at first sight.

John muttered something profane but incoherent in reply, and flung a sulky nod to the knot of loafers in the veranda, who, having been drinking at his expense since Friday, returned it with an interest not dissociated from satire. Then he was off at a brisk canter, sitting, as someone unkindly observed, "like a sack of coals"; and, though sitting close, swaying in the saddle every few strides, in clear indication that his balance was as yet imperfect.

Tenements, whether wood or canvas, were few enough at King Parrot Flat; but what there were lay wide apart on either side the broad bush highway, divided by clumps of gum and belts of wattle and wild fern; so that the township, which could have been set down in three or four acres just as well, extended from end to end nearly a mile. As Jake passed close in front of

49

the opposition grog-shanty at the other side of the road, higher up, he was playfully hooted by a second — naturally hostile — knot of loafers. Outside Harrison's store, still higher up, the aged Harrison, who was sunning himself in front of the house, laid down his newspaper and broke into a cackle of senile mirth as the odd horseman — whom he took for an Australian John Gilpin — thundered past. And little Martha Byrne, driving back the cows from the creek, made such an impudent, impish grimace in his very path, that Long Jake turned in the saddle with a more savage look upon John Byrne's child than he had hurled back at the grown men. Even the cows stood still to regard him with bland astonishment, as he clattered through their midst. There was only one house left to pass — a long, low, new building, more pretentious than any other in the township. It was the new store, lately opened by new arrivals in the colony; the bold venture of a young immigrant couple, and so far held in supreme contempt by the broad spirits of King Parrot Flat. Mrs Truscott — the township said unanimously — *might* be a fine young woman; they weren't so sure about that, however; but one thing they were sure about — she would have to get rid of those confounded "old-country airs" of hers before they had anything to do either with her, or her stuck-up husband. As for the latter, why, he actually thought he knew something about horses; as if as new chum in the colony *could* know anything about horses! And he had a young colt or two up there in his yards that he was breaking in, English fashion. Just fancy trying on that kind of "rot" with bush-horses! King Parrot Flat thought it all an excellent joke, though one which — as men of "savvy" — they could not help feeling strongly about.

Now the road to Razorback twisted abruptly round the corner of this Truscott's store; and after passing the store, Jake would be alike beyond the township and range of those arrows of ridicule to which an unsteady rider presents a gratuitous target. He therefore made no attempt to check his pace as he swept round close to the picket-fence in front of Truscott's veranda. Had he done so, he might have heard and understood the bounding thuds of a bucking horse, close at hand, before he doubled the angle of the fence and before it was too late to prevent a collision; for Truscott had mounted a vicious young brute that was at that moment bucking furiously. As it was, before either rider could utter a cry, the horses met. Jake was thrown clear and far; and as ground and sky whirled before him, the last thing he saw was the young hose reared, as it seemed, into the dark-blue vault overhead — trembling in the balance — falling backward.

Jake was only half-stunned by the fall, but he was more than half-sobered. In an instant he had picked himself up. The colt was just rising to his legs, apparently no worse; his own mare was cantering awkwardly away, with her near foreleg thrust through the reins; and on the ground, close to the stockyard rail, lay a heap of gray flannel and white moleskin and quivering flesh. At sight of this, alcohol seemed to reassert its sway in Jake's brain; it reeled; and he was hardly more conscious of what followed than of what took place around him while he was lying helpless and insensate at John Byrne's.

Twenty minutes later, the rushing air on his temples brought him once more to his sober senses. He was on the mare, and was riding swiftly back to the hut. Then, for the second time that day, Long Jake tried to piece together what had happened. But now all came back to him consecutively and with fearful vividness: How he had crept timidly up to the thing that lay so still, touched it, and started back; lifted an arm, and let it drop heavily. How he had taken the warm yet lifeless body in his arms, and, exerting all his strength, staggered with it round to the veranda, where a shrieking, laughing maniac had rushed out upon him. How, in spite of the madwoman, he had borne in his burden and laid it down as gently as might be. How, very soon, a noisy rabble rushed up; how he had answered their questions as clearly as he could, and promised to return to the township if wanted; and was then suffered to break away. All as in a dream.

But that night, when safely back at his shepherd's hut, away on the sloping pasture-land beyond Razorback, when darkness fell over all things, and the white dead gum-trees towered like risen spectres on the side of the range — that night, Long Jake lay tossing on his bunk and making sure that this time, at last, delirium tremens had fairly caught him. For the moon, shooting her cold rays through the open door of the hut, cast a ghostly white shadow on the sandy floor — a gleaming ghostly shadow, sliced as with a knife out of the surrounding blackness, and taking the hideous shape of a coffin; and outside, the young saplings were nodding their heads like funeral plumes; and the crickets croaking a hoarse, monotonous, maddening dirge. Then soon the dead face of the man was thrust before his disordered vision; and anon the frantic face of the woman. So that at last he could bear it no longer, but tore himself from the bunk, and roamed through the night, half-dressed as he was, among the pale corpses of trees, until the morning dew upon his uncovered head, and the morning breeze upon his fevered temples, helped to cool and clear the poor bewildered brain.

Long Jake was in the habit of planning these systematic carousels of his with a deliberation that was little short of horrible. This time he had waited patiently until heavy rain filled the creeks and water-holes, so that his flocks had the best of feed and water close at hand; and he had trimmed and

52

mended the rude fences of the great paddocks, and left everything generally snug. Then he had obtained from his employer a substantial cheque, on the pretext of buying a horse at Wattledown. For the projected "bust" was by no means Jake's first since his installation in the hut on Razorback, and he was well aware that if he were found out — let alone the harm that might or might not befall the sheep during his absence — it would be at least as much as his place was worth: *that* was thirty shillings a week, plus rations, and in itself was of small consideration; he could get as much, perhaps more, from any squatter in the colony, as an experienced shepherd and boundary-man. But somehow, Jake had got to like the place for its own sake. He was content in his solitary life among the grim and sombre ranges. Indeed, this queer, reserved, nameless old fellow found the solitude of Razorback the best thing in life. I am not sure that he did not regard those "bursts" at King Parrot Flat simply as so many necessary life-tonics which he owed it to himself to administer with unfailing regularity. At any rate the rude slab hut, the cats, the cockatoo, the very prints pasted on the walls — these simple signs grew by degrees to spell for Long Jake the word "Home". And until this time he had experienced nothing but thankfulness and relief on returning home, sick and wearied, from his excesses.

But this time it was different. Home conveyed no comfort; he could not rest. He felt that which, out of a pretty lengthy experience of smaller after-glows, he had never felt before — namely, shame. That was not the worst of it, however. The dead storekeeper was always before his eyes. And when riding through the bush, he found himself unconsciously looking over his shoulder, fearfully expectant of the wild face and uplifted arm of the woman who he had been instrumental in making a widow. For brooding exaggerated the circumstances of the accident, until the brand of the primal murderer would burn on the face of Long Jake in the dead of night and send the poor self-accuser wandering pitifully over the ranges.

Rough as the life was in the old days — the other time-honoured epithet is for the optimists — there were still coroners to be had for the sending, even in the ranges. And a couple of days after the accident, a messenger summoned Long Jake to the inquest at the dead man's store. Well, no blame was laid upon poor Jake, except by himself; and he galloped back without speaking to a soul outside the store. The widow could not be brought to attend the inquiry, and she was not seen.

A part of the weight that pressed it down was now lifted from the mind of Long Jake, but only a slight part. In the distorted perspective of his own mind he was still blood-guilty; and could there be degrees in blood-guiltiness? He would have ridden into the home-station and laid bare his naked feelings to the boss, who was a kind and just man, and who, moreover, would certainly hear of the accident from other — possibly unkind — lips. But, unfortunately, the one rigid rule of Long Jake's life was, never to lay bare a fraction of his feelings to a fellow-man. However, after a few days, a journey to the homestead, for rations, became imperative. It was high noon when, amid a loud barking of dogs, Jake led his mare into the rough stable and walked over to the store. Within, the young gentleman from England — who was obliging enough to acquire "colonial experience" at a nominal salary — was whistling shrilly.

"Ha! it's you, Long Jake," he cried, as Jake entered. "Rations? All right; in a minute; but — hang it — shake a paw first, do." He was evidently in tremendous spirits; and Jake was too perfectly colonised to be in sympathy with any such demonstration. He held out his hand sulkily; he intended to have his rations at once, and go. But the high-spirited young

54

gentleman went on whistling noisily and packing emu eggs in sawdust, as if no one was at the other side of the counter waiting to be served.

"Tell you what's up," he presently volunteered, pausing in his song; "I'm off home! Sick o' this, don't you know — rough as blazes, and all that kind of thing. Yes, home to England! Jolly, eh?" A vivacious continuation of the interrupted tune, in another key, and then: "Sail next Tuesday week; Blackwall liner; good business, eh?" Crescendo: the whole store filled with the volume of this young Briton's whistle.

"If it's a fair question," asked Jake, when the tune had come to a blatant end on a wrong note, "what might a passage cost?"

"Just the sort of question it is — ha, ha! — you don't see it, though!" laughed the other airily. "Why, about seventy pounds, first-class."

"Ah, but second?"

"Oh, about thirty, I should say. Why? Are you thinking of going home too?"

Jake said curtly that he wasn't; and asked plainly if he might expect to be served that morning.

While the young man was busy with the scales, William Noble — "the boss" — came into the store and conversed pleasantly with his boundary-man without one allusion to King Parrot Flat. And before he left the homestead, Long Jake ascertained that he had still five pounds seventeen and eightpence standing to his credit in the station books.

"Thirty pounds!" he muttered strangely as he resumed the mare. He had "lammed down" that sum at John Byrne's the week before! He rode home to the hut in silent thought; but when he dismounted at the well-known spot, he once more whispered, "Thirty pounds!" This time the words fell naturally from his lips; they had formed the keynote of his reflections during the ten-mile ride.

More than three months passed before Long Jake was again seen at King Parrot Flat; and then, one fine afternoon, he dropped in upon the boys in John Byrne's bar without a word of warning. He was warmly greeted. John Byrne's handsome face lit up with an evil light as he clapped the newcomer on the back with demonstrative heartiness; Jack Rogers, already three parts tipsy, foresaw earlier consummation than he had dared to hope for; and Surgeon-major Wagstaff — late of H.M. Bombay Staff Corps — deemed it a promising speculation to begin business by pledging Long Jake at his, the Surgeon-major's, expense. To the speechless amazement of all, this delicate overture was politely but promptly declined.

"No, boys," said Long Jake quietly, in answer to the questioning faces that were turned indignantly to his; "I ha'n't come here for a boose — not this time"; and he calmly seated himself on a flour-bag in the coolest corner of the store.

Jack Rogers feebly appealed to his stars to explain what this might portend; the old Anglo-Indian opened with much more than tropic rapidity from pink to purple, and muttered vaguely about "outraged honour" and "instant satisfaction"; while the proprietor of the bar confined himself to a peremptory inquiry as to why, et cetera, Jake came there if he didn't mean to take anything for the good of the house — adding that he, for one, as boss of the shanty in question, intended to know the reason why, anyway.

"Reason why?" said Long Jake reflectively, without looking up from the fig of tobacco he was daintily pairing in his palm. "Reason why? Why, to have a bit of a yarn. What else?" But before the menace that trembled on John Byrne's tongue could be discharged, he added adroitly, and with a quick upward glance: "Hows'ever, though I'm not on for anything myself today — feeling just what you call below par, like — I hereby invites all present company to order their usual, if *you* please." With that Long Jake added to the painful interest which his abnormal conduct had already created by shifting the clasp-knife to his left hand, thrusting his right deep into his trousers' pocket, and, apparently by accident, jingling a fistful of coins. Then he withdrew his hand without raising his eyes, and resumed paring the tobacco with an impassive face.

Coin of the realm being an almost unknown quantity at King Parrot Flat, where paper-money was in common currency, this master-touch of Long Jake's produced an instantaneous effect. John Byrne turned his back, partly to uncork a fresh demijohn, partly to conceal his emotion. The rest — including even the insulted Surgeon-major — maintained a judicious silence. The man from Razorback reserved his final bomb until the first glass all round had been emptied, and until he had rolled his tobacco caressingly between his palms, and filled and lit his pipe.

"Fact is, boys," he then said, in the same calm deliberate tone, "I'm going home."

The silence that had preceded the announcement outlived it half a minute; then, as one man, the *habitués* of Byrne's bar pulled themselves together. "What! — home to England?" asked John Byrne incredulously.

"Gad! You don't mean this?" exclaimed Surgeon-major Wagstaff.

"My colonial oath on it," said Long Jake.

"An' when yer goin'?" inquired Jack Rogers.

"Well, not *jest* yet a while," said Long Jake.

This last reply, being distinctly anti-climacteric, disappointed somewhat.

57

"Going for good?" sneered John Byrne, veiling beneath a tone of contempt the reasonable annoyance incident to loss of a sure source of income. Jack Rogers, with a vinous wink, suggested: "No; for bad." A slight laugh greeted the maudlin sally. But Jake replied gravely: "Only for a trip. I mean to have one more look at the old dust; that's all. Fill up again, boys!"

The invitation was scarcely needed; and, under the influence of the whiskey and Jake's maneuvring, the conversation drifted; and he presently turned it into the channel he had all along in view by an innocent inquiry after Widow Truscott. The gratuitous information respecting this lady which he elicited it would be to no purpose to relate at length; moreover, it would be unfair, since the epithets employed could scarcely have been meant for repetition. But it did appear that Mrs Truscott was, to put it mildly, no favourite at King Parrot Flat. Her airs were worse than ever. She thought herself too good for everybody. She was mismanaging the store, making a mess of everything, and doing no business — each substantive being duly qualified. There were plenty of good men ready to enter the business on the square footing, who would guarantee to make a paying concern of it. Yet she wanted to sell the place — sell a place whose goodwill wasn't worth a red cent; she would look at none of them. Here the gallant Surgeon-major waxed peculiarly eloquent and pompous. It seemed that this oriental jewel had indeed gone the length of personally offering himself, body and soul, as a sacrifice at the shrine of this unreasonable woman. Only to be trampled on!

As Long Jake cantered homeward, he could not resist a curious glance at the dwelling of the terrible female. If she treated so maleficiently these estimable men, whose worst offence was a too great admiration for herself, how would she behave to him, Long Jake — the author, as he persisted in regarding himself, of her widowhood? Might she not send a bullet through him as he passed? Surely she must be capable of that much. She happened to be in front of the house, training lovingly an infant creeper to the base of a veranda-post — honeysuckle, taken from its native soil only a few short months ago. She looked up swiftly at the cantering horseman. As it seemed to him, there was nothing forbidding in the glance; nor did she lower her eyes; but, instead, gazed hard at him with something very like interest in her sad face. Long Jake felt the blood mount hotly to his cheeks, and his hand tighten involuntarily on the reins. For an instant he wavered; then, turning away his head, he spurred the mare round the fatal corner. But he had not galloped a furlong before his first impulse of shame gave place to one of indignation, of which he himself was the object; he fell to cursing himself for a fool and a heartless wretch; and by the time he reached the hut, he had resolved that, next time anything took him to the township, he would not leave it before he had told the truth to the poor widow about that terrible day, now nearly four months ago.

It was a little curious that, hardly a week later, Long Jake found another trip to King Parrot Flat necessary. He had never before visited the township twice in so short a space of time. It was more curious, however, that he ended by getting no farther than the outermost *vedette* of the straggling, weather-board houses — by calling in, in fine, at Mrs Truscott's store and nowhere else.

"I must see the woman; I must make a clean breast to her about that day. I must tell her straight that I was blind drunk and riding madly; that if I had been in my sober senses, the accident would never have happened." Such is a paraphrase and a condensation of Long Jake's conception of his duty, arrived at after hours of slow laborious thought. The logic of the conclusion was more than questionable; and as for the prompting that led to it, Jake was simply self-deceived. Even supposing any good sprang up from the unburdening of spirit, it would be reaped by the wrong person; a load would be lifted from Long Jake's heart, not a pennyweight from Mrs Truscott's. Yet, as he reined up at the store, Long Jake honestly believed that he was about to do the next best thing to reparation, which was impossible. Mrs Truscott sat sewing behind the green veranda-blinds — voluptuous extravagances hitherto unknown in the pure air of the Flat. The tall ungainly bushman trembled visibly as he stepped up the little path, crushing his soft wideawake between the twitching fingers of both hands. Instantly, however, the sweet, sad smile with which the young widow looked up at his troubled face disarmed him; that ice-breaking sentence, so carefully prepared, so often rehearsed, went clean out of his head; and Long Jake, for one faint-hearted moment, would have given far more than his credit balance at the station to be safely back in his hut!

Yet a moment later the plunge was made — a veritable flounder of incoherence. Then, coming up — so to speak — for breath, a series of verbal splashes followed, tremulous with rough pent-up emotion; for some seconds the words chased each other tumultuously from his hoarse throat, then ceased. And the widow knew all that had been on the poor fellow's mind for months past.

How did she bear it? Silently, at first; then with a slight catch of the breath; then with quiet tears. And when all was said, she leant forward on her low chair and pronounced, not forgiveness, but words of thanks. Thanks to him! The man recoiled, and shuddered, and refused to believe his ears. He felt stunned, when no reproach could have stunned him! But a thin white hand was stretched over toward him, and, whether he would or no, it buried itself in his great coarse fist. He

60

dropped it quickly, drew a deep sigh, half of relief, half of bewilderment, wiped his shirt-sleeve across his brow, and without a word, stepped from the veranda.

Mrs Truscott called him back. He must stay a little while, she said kindly, and talk to her: she never talked to anyone, you see. Jake sat down humbly; he would have done anything she told him, just then; but what could he talk about? Silence. Jake shifted nervously. Some subtle instinct whispered that he would be evermore disgraced if he left the lady to begin the conversation. So he stumbled into this: "I'm goin' to clear out o' this soon."

The widow looked up from her needle-work in surprise, as well she might. "How do you mean?" asked she, not without apprehension.

"These here ranges; I'm going to leave 'em."

"Yes?" — in a tone indicating interest.

"Yes" — in one betraying exhaustion of topic.

"And where do you go then?"

"Ha!" with unexpected relief, and surprise that he should have forgotten what was indeed his point — "home to England!"

Mrs Truscott dropped her work on her lap, and looked swiftly up at the speaker. And for a single moment — in spite of her thin worn cheeks, in spite of the lines that had come ten years before their time — for that one moment the parted lips, the wide-open blue eyes, the sudden flash of strong interest, lit up the woman's face into beauty. The next, the blue eyes filled with tears, the chin drooped, the cheeks went paler than before, and a broken voice repeated in a wondering whisper: "Home to England!"

"Yes," said Long Jake softly; "home! For a trip."

But he had no sooner uttered the words than he jumped up clumsily without a word of warning and stepped hastily out of the veranda. Almost instantaneously, Mrs Truscott heard a shrill exclamation, followed by a volley of angry words.

"Why, whatever is it? Ah, dear, dear, dear!" she cried, rushing out, with something akin to a fresh pang in her heart.

"It's only this, ma'am," he cried savagely, throwing out a dramatic arm in the direction of a dark little figure that was racing rapidly down the broad bush high-road towards the other houses; "that there little snake has been a-hiding behind this here picket-fence and a-listening to every word you and me has been a-saying. Confound her!"

The widow turned; and, though the evening gloom was settling rapidly, it needed but a glance to assure her that yonder skeltering imp was the one human creature in the township in whom she took any sort of interest — little Martha Byrne, whom she had even attempted to teach to read. The hot blood mounted to the woman's faded face. She faced about. But Long Jake was gone. Growing momently fainter, his mare's rhythmical canter was borne to Mrs Truscott's ears as the strokes rang out from the flint-strewn track. The widow sighed deeply. Every breath she drew was a sigh; but this one came with new force from a new pain; or rather, from an ever-present pain re-awakened.

"Poor thing!" said Jake aloud, as the mare dropped into a walk at the foot of the steep winding track over Razorback. "No sign of business, as I could see. Why, the place was never fairly started. Poor thing!"

Nearly an hour later, he put the mare into a canter at the top of the long gentle slope that stretched, though miles of timber, right down to the hut; and then he was thinking of that look of Mrs Truscott's when he spoke the word "Home!" "Ay, she'd go home too, fast enough, if she had the money," thought Jake.

With the quickened stride of the mare, the rider's thoughts, too, came the quicker. At first he made no effort to check them; but presently he found himself spurring on the mare in order to leave them far behind. The grotesquely-twisted gums fled by on either hand, bowing mockingly in the evening breeze as he passed; then the round moon shot up and painted the narrow track an ashy gray, and threw into merciless relief, among a world of phantoms, one solitary mortal flying from a Thought. But the Thought was not to be run away from. It twined its tendrils about the man's mind, and grew and grew until he became hardly conscious of the trees rushing by; the long gray track reeling out beneath, the scent of the eucalyptus forest tingling in his nostrils. Suddenly a peal of harsh grating laughter broke upon the silence. The rider instinctively pulled up. The hoarse diabolical peal was repeated; but this time it was echoed by a low chuckle from Long Jake. He had lived in the bush more years than he could count; yet here, forsooth, he was startled by the bushman's familiar, the laughing-jackass! The momentary sensation, however, had an immediate effect: Long Jake shook himself together and rode slowly and soberly forward. Not that the Thought was expelled; it was to remain, but on a different footing; for now it was no longer resisted, but willingly, coolly, discriminately entertained.

Before starting on the rounds of his paddocks next morning, Long Jake made a calculation with the butt-end of his stock-whip on the sandy soil outside the hut door. When the sum was worked out, he stamped out the figures, as if ashamed. Yet he had merely satisfied himself that in three months' time his gross savings would amount to pretty nearly fifty pounds. "And on that," said Long Jake slowly, "and on what the mare brings, we *might* manage it."

The spring months that followed were trying ones to Long Jake. He never went near King Parrot Flat. One or two trips he made over to Wattletown, in order to negotiate for the sale of the mare with a storekeeper there, which ended in a bargain being struck that the mare should be delivered and paid for by Christmas at the latest; but on these occasions Wattletown observed that the man from Razorback conducted himself very meanly, and that the little money he did spend was in hard cash. In point of fact he made it his first business to cash a small cheque at the bank on entering the township. Then, of course, there were the inevitable visits to the home-station. But only two circumstances happened really to break the monotony of life, which, after years and years of it, became actively unpalatable to Long Jake's temperament for the first time. The first of these was a visit from handsome John Byrne, who slept at the hut on his way to the home-station, where — so he said — he had business with Mr Noble; though, in fact — which he omitted to add — he paid Jake the compliment of travelling many miles out of his way in order to see him, since he came straight from the lair of a lynx-eyed congenial sprit at Wattletown, and not from the grog-shanty on the Flat. The visitor, however, was too welcome for Long Jake to consider the visit mysterious; and as for sinister glances and cunning questions, Jake neither saw the first, nor was even aware that the second had been put — and answered.

The other circumstance was this: one day he found lying in the station store an envelope addressed to "The Boundary-man on Razorback". It contained a few lines from Mrs Truscott, begging Jake to call at her store before his departure for England, provided he should consent to be the bearer of a message and a trifle or two besides. He spelt through the note with difficulty, then laboriously indited a reply and dropped it into the mail-bag. In his note a day in December was mentioned on which he would without fail present himself at Mrs Truscott's service. After that, with a feeling of satisfaction quite new to him, he inquired for the boss. Mr Noble, who had already heard with amusement of Jake's projected trip home, was not surprised to hear now that he intended coming in for his cheque about the middle of December. Jake, however, promised to stay until a new boundary-rider should be sent out to the hut, which, it was in turn promised, should be done a day or two before that on which he wished expressly to leave.

As December drew gradually nearer, he grew daily wearier of his daily work. He became restlessly impatient; and his nights were broken by vivid, disturbing dreams. As a rule these dreams bore him back across seas of time and the world to a peaceful little hamlet in Somersetshire. But they invariably ended by the distant and indistinct image of the English village fading before the strong, convincing presentment of King Parrot Flat; or the two places would be fused fantastically together, as is the way with dream-locality.

When at length the great day dawned, Jake set out for the station at sunrise, riding the mare, and carrying all his personal belongings in the swag strapped across the saddle. At the station, Jake received his breakfast and his cheque; the latter — the account coming to a few pounds under fifty — being written for that round sum, thanks to a graceful bonus from the boss. Thus emancipated, Jake rode on to Wattletown with a heart of air, leading a station horse which Noble lent him for the completion of his roundabout journey to King Parrot Flat. At Wattletown, the mare was sold, according to the previous arrangement, for twenty pounds down in cash. The cheque also was cashed — all gold; so that when Jake rode away from that prosperous settlement at four in the afternoon he had seventy sovereigns in the leather pouch on his belt, which was imprudent, in spite of his modest conviction that not a soul was concerned — and therefore, he argued, not a soul could be

65

acquainted — with the movements of so obscure an individual as Long Jake.

After an hour's easy riding, Jake was once more on thoroughly familiar ground; for halfway between the Flat and his old hut that track was joined by the one from Wattletown. Never had this man's spirits been so high before, never had the sombre tint of the bush seemed so warm and gay in the glinting sunlight. The gray rough track had never bounded so lightly from the heels of the good old mare; though surely this heavy bony hack was not a patch upon her for speed and lightness. The excitement that had entered his spirit during the last months had given new life and animation to a narrow, silent, well-nigh animal existence. He was no longer the thing that repeatedly, for days, lay helpless at Byrne's bar, and returned to the hut he called home without pang, without a regret, without a hope. And here it was, in these endless cloisters of smooth round trunks, that the Thought had come to him which had worked all this wondrous change — the Thought that was now at last to be put to the test, whether it was wise or unwise, good or evil!

"Ha, ha! Ha, ha!"

Ah! that could startle him *then*, but not now! Long Jake turned round in the saddle to look at the queer clumsy bird — surely a bird of good omen. But he did not slacken his steady canter.

"Ha, ha, ha!"

This time the laugh did not come from behind. Jake turned sharply. Directly in the track sat a tall, motionless, masked figure on horseback; and a voice that Jake thought he recognised cried: "Bale up!"

"Bale up!" — the seventy sovereigns! Jake's heart quailed and sickened for a moment. The long barrel of a revolver covered him, and glittered in the sunlight. Must he be robbed

66

in broad daylight? With a wild cry of rage and despair, he buried his spurs in the sides of his heavy mount and dashed straight at the highwayman, leaning forward with his face on the horse's mane. The robber, being less heavily mounted, backed a pace; and as Long Jake came on armed and reckless, took deliberate aim at the chest of the charging horse. A firm quick touch on the reins caused the heavy brute to swerve, and with a loud ring the bullet struck the near stirrup-iron, thence burying itself in the heel of Jake's boot. The frightened animal thundered on; and in an instant they were past, nearly bringing the smaller horse to earth in their rush. A quick succession of shots and an even louder volley of curses filled the air; Long Jake felt a stinging, burning blow between the shoulder-blades; his brain sickened, and his body reeled in the saddle!

Just as the fiery sun began to dip behind the range, Mrs Truscott heard a furious clatter of hoofs outside. She rose hastily and ran out. So did Martha Byrne, whom the widow had tried in vain to get rid of all the afternoon. Staggering through the little wicket-gate was a strange figure, all dust and sweat and blood, and the ashiest face man ever reeled under. He made his way unsteadily up to the veranda, where he sank down with a deep sobbing sigh; and his head would have fallen back upon the boards had not the widow caught his shoulders and supported him. His breath came quick and short, his eyes seemed closing; yet his fingers fumbled feebly until they had unfastened a leather pouch from his belt. And then his hands were powerless to lift it!

The stricken man looked dumbly upward at the woman; he could just raise a trembling pointing hand to her, then drop it significantly on the pouch. His lips moved, and from between them came one faint word: "Home!"

Little Martha had for once used her long thin legs to some purpose. After one quick intelligent glance at the pallid face of Long Jake, she had rushed like the wind to her father's shanty; and now she was returning, almost as swiftly, with a posse of its choice spirits. John Byrne was absent, and mysteriously absent, from the township; but foremost among them was Surgeon-major Wagstaff, carrying his instrument case and a vastly augmented pomposity of bearing; and devoutly hoping that, whoever the fellow was, he would live long enough to give him (Wagstaff) a show of getting his hand in once more. Jack Rogers was there too, and Paddy Welch, and one or two others. With the carmine glare of the setting sun behind them, the two figures that met their gaze seemed of carved ebony, both were so black and so rigid! As one man, the little party slackened its pace; Paddy Welch doffed his felt wideawake, and the others did the same; then they moved forward very, very slowly. And Jack Rogers said, just above his breath, but, somehow, more gruffly than he intended to say it: "He's gone home square enough now, boys; *and for good!*"

Yet darkness fell over King Parrot Flat, and the boys still lingered outside the window of Truscott's store. For the Surgeon-major said there was still the ghost of a chance; and the Surgeon-major was sober and on his mettle, and ought to have known, even if he didn't.

That day week they ran John Byrne to earth in the ranges. They dragged him back to the Flat, and would have lynched him in sight of his own bar, but for one circumstance. The ink was scarcely dry on an official bulletin nailed to the door of the now flourishing opposition shanty which set forth that the patient was definitely out of danger. And they found its author, the gallant and skilful Surgeon-major, already gloriously drunk after his week of enforced sobriety by the sick man's bed.

So Mr John Byrne, amateur bushranger, was taken over to Wattletown and handed over, quite nicely, to the police. Thanks to a woman's nursing and a Surgeon-major's experience, Long Jake pulled through. Just when the days began to shorten, and camping on Razorback became mean work, the shutters were put up at the new store. A week later, Long Jake's trip home began. But Jake Rogers turned out quite right after all: the trip was confessedly "for good". Nor was it made alone.

Miss Teague's Behaviour

When the eldest Miss Teague got engaged to be married, she startled the parish and delighted a greater number of persons than are usually affected by the happiness of one. Also it looked as if she had broken a certain undesirable spell; at any rate the second Miss Teague was wooed and married within that year.

Now the Misses Teagues' father — the respected rector of Rix — might or might not have been able to tell you, offhand, how many Miss Teagues there were. All he cared to remember was that he had one son, to succeed to the living. His future was assured, and indeed he was already a rector in his own right, elsewhere, for the time being. But what future had the girls if they did not marry? They had no money of their own; neither they nor their father had any notion of their making any; such notions do not travel to places like Rix. They had no mother. They saw very few young men. It was really wonderful how one of them had become engaged and another actually married. But the younger ones did not follow suit; and the younger ones were not so very young; yet all they did was to play tennis very hard, dance whenever they could, have the greatest fun among themselves in the school-room and take life at all points less seriously than their eldest sister, who was in for a long engagement.

Miss Teague, whose name was Caroline, was perhaps a thought too serious; but then she had serious responsibilities to fulfil — it had been so from her earliest girlhood. She kept house at the rectory, played the organ in church and did more in the parish than the rector himself.

It would be a difficult task to describe Miss Teague, for the reason that her beauty was largely spiritual. It lay in her large, clear gray eyes, so kind, trustful and sympathetic. You could look through and through her, at least a keen judge of human nature could. Thinking well of everybody, she had no reason for concealing her thoughts. She didn't know that she was so honest. The harmony of her nature was like the song-bird's melody — poured out rather machine like. She was one of those women who find it easier to trust people than doubt them. And yet Caroline was not devoid of physical grace and beauty. Tall, slender and with an exquisite complexion, a trifle pale, perhaps, but strangely white and perfect, a great wealth of dark chestnut hair and teeth unusually free of blemish or defect — all these added to that charm which lay in the trustful gaze of those large, gray eyes.

It need hardly be said that she was very much liked in Rix, and that she was devoted to the people. In the school-room at home she was looked up to rather, and admired, of course, but she sometimes felt she spoilt the fun there. She was less noisy than the rest, and sensibly older; she was older than their brother even, who made a gap between her and the younger ones which Fanny's marriage had sensibly widened. The girls hardly looked on Caroline as one of themselves; she had such unattractive interests, and her tennis was not up to their level. There was no part for her, really, in their amusements — though they appreciated her presence and applause "in front". And if they were more bent upon enjoyment than she was, and if they did let her stay at home nearly always, when only so many could go to this or that, were they not much younger than Caroline, and was not Caroline engaged? Her engagement was never lost sight of in the school-room, though one might have known Miss Teague rather well without suspecting that the brisk, unselfish creature was in love.

It was a long engagement, certainly. Caroline had become used to her engagement ring before Fanny met her fate at the county tournament; and Caroline caressed Fanny's baby, as Miss Teague still, with shapeless feelings which she herself but imperfectly understood . She had been engaged for three years, and for eighteen months she had not seen him. He was a clergyman, too, the Rev. Noel Pennyman. He had a pedigree, I believe, but it would have been better if he had possessed some private means; as it was, he had taken a curacy at the other end of England, where he was working very zealously in a busy, grimy city. His letters came regularly twice a week to the lazy, rustic rectory at Rix — letters from another world. They were always interesting and amusing and written with care in Pennyman's pretty, scholarly hand, and Caroline, though so alert and practical, had her own spot in the old garden where she used to read them three seasons out of four, while even happier hours were spent in her own room late at night in answering these letters.

"No, we are going to wait till Noel has a living," she used firmly to reply to inquisitive friends. "We're perfectly resigned, thank you. It would be intolerable to marry now, on the little he has — I mean it would make Noel miserable. He is working tremendously in his parish, and I am in mine, you know, and we're both content to wait. He is certain to get something some day if he sticks to that diocese. Do I wish he were nearer? Well, I should like to know the people he is among, certainly; he tells me all about them. I know their names, but I should like to know them. It will all come right in the end. Noel is very sensible about it — you don't know how sensible he is — so surely I can be too. You see, we are neither of us chickens!"

Her face shone when she spoke of him. It was true that they were not boy and girl; but Caroline, as a matter of fact, was the

72

elder of the two. As for Pennyman, he was an Oxford friend of young Teague and had stayed many times at the rectory before he proposed to Caroline, or paid her particular attention even. The affair seemed rather sudden at the time; but everybody was glad about it, and we know that it broke a most evil spell. It was a pity, of course, that Pennyman's distinguished family were neither wealthy nor connected to the church by any more influential link than Pennyman. But Pennyman was clever and hard-working as well as handsome, tall and dashing, and preferment was certain to come in time. Meanwhile he was particularly sensible. He was engaged to a young woman who would make an ideal clergyman's wife — who would assist him immensely in his parish — who had his views — who was as well up in the whole thing as he was himself — who was entirely in love with him. He could well afford to wait. He was too sensible even to quarrel with the irritating set of circumstances that kept them apart for eighteen months. He wrote his neat, entertaining, sensible letters the whole time — and one, at the end, that brought tears of joy to Caroline's wide, gray eyes.

She took it to the rector in his study and told him, very simply, that at last Noel could come, if they could do with him. Of course they could do with him; and the proud old parson, leaning back from his desk, kissed his daughter in kind congratulations.

"But, dear me," said he, "how long it is since he was last here — what a time he has been up yonder! Really, he ought to be getting something better; he deserves it, I am sure. Do you think he looks out enough?"

"Dear father," said Caroline, in her gentle way, "he is very fond of his work up there; he loves it and the people, and of course they are devoted to him. You know, we look at it very sensibly. You shall marry us some day!"

73

"I am ready when you are, my dear," said the rector, dryly. His spectacles were levelled at the buttercups and daisies through the open widow. He was rather serious. "And I must say I shall be glad when you ready. You have been engaged three years — it is a long business. I shall miss you dreadfully, Caroline, and there is no one to fill your place — I realise that. But I want to see you happy, my child — I do want to see you happy!"

"Father! I can never be happier than I am now," cried Caroline, with her whole heart. But she left the rector still thoughtfully regarding the unshorn lawn. He was looking back at his own case, perhaps! He had married on a curacy, and a poor one, long before his succession to the family living. In his day, in fact, as he remembered it, young people who wanted one another had not been so sensible.

Miss Teague carried her good news to the school-room, for she had not opened the letter until after breakfast in the usual place. The room was the school-room in name only now, and the laughter and high spirits within made Caroline pause in self-conscious trepidation before opening the door. When she did go in, however, the girls were perfectly sweet about it. They threw down their work — they did a little work in the mornings sometimes, it is fair to say — and were honestly and noisily delighted. And Miss Teague, smiling and blushing in their midst, looked almost as pretty, just then, as her pretty sisters. In reality she was no such thing: she had beautiful hair, and good, gray eyes, and there was character in her mouth. But her sisters were pretty, and much younger.

Caroline had told her father she could never be happier than she was then: and perhaps the fortnight that intervened between the receipt of Noel Pennyman's delightful news and that young clergyman's actual arrival was the happiest time she had ever known. She spent it in the cloudless nook of anticipation. He

74

was coming again, the man it was her pride to love, and she had not even seen him for a year and a half. She wondered how the time had passed, now she looked back upon it. She shuddered at the thought of another such a term of separation and divided labour and patiently waiting and faith and hope. Yet her home life was particularly full, interesting and responsible. She had believed formerly that nothing under heaven could induce her to leave home and Rix; but that was before she knew Noel Pennyman well. Now it was her proud desire to give up all she loved as dearly for him she loved more dearly still. Her love was of a sacrificial sort. What it cost her, it was her pride to suffer; infinite delay, long separations, the unsettling intermediate state of the betrothed, and all attendant pangs she suffered eagerly for his sake — as eagerly as she worked stoles and vestments for his person. She considered it her blessed privilege to wait and suffer and work (when she could) for Noel, but she did not go about saying so. You could see it in her face but her happiness was too genuine to need, or even to allow, ingenious explanation. Her best friends never heard her say that she had realised her ideal in this and that respect. Probably she had done so in all respects. But this never occurred to her in so many thoughts. She loved.

Her love added lustre to a life already shining with a kindly light. It beamed upon those privileged souls who peopled her little, happy world. It made the large soft heart of Caroline Teague softer and larger yet. It widened her sympathies. It broadened her mind. It gave to her fingers, even, on the organ keys a tender, soulful touch which some loving listeners discovered that they had missed in her playing hitherto.

Now that he was coming again, after so long an absence, these kind signs increased and were intensified. But Miss Teague did some quite weak things in private. She surveyed herself in the glass, repeatedly, one might say exhaustively.

She gave more thought to her dress than she had ever given before.

Hitherto the idea had scarcely ever suggested itself to Miss Teague that a woman could by a careful and intelligent study of her complexion and figure, of her peculiar style, as it is tritely termed, increase the charm of her personality. She would have been loath to admit that a young woman had any right to attract a man's attention by leading him to think she was possessed of either a moral or a physical beauty when in reality she was not. To Caroline deception in any form or to any degree, no matter how slight, was abhorrent. Even to gain a fortune or a man's love she could not have brought herself to lend her skin an additional softness and whiteness by dusting it with powder.

But when her thoughts reverted to her betrothed, it suddenly floated upon her mind that possibly he had changed, possibly during these many months he had been thrown among so-called fashionable young women who study modes with a real intensity of application, who follow the styles, who are thoroughly informed as to every new discovery in the art of decorating and beautifying the person, and for the first time it occurred to her that she was what is commonly denominated a plain girl, while he was a tall, handsome, dashing man very little like what his calling would lead one to suppose him to be, and no doubt, too, he was popular with women. How could it be otherwise? Handsome men were sure to be flattered and feted and made much of. It often spoiled them, too, for they were, in spite of their pretension to being the stronger vessel, quite as puffed up with social success, quite as prone to be undone by excessive commendation as the weaker vessel. In fact, even more so, for the reason that their famed security afforded them by their stronger minds really made them rush more quickly into danger. And yet they were but mortal, born

76

of woman, with not even woman's lofty sense of duty to restrain them.

Caroline's thoughts absolutely startled her. She had never before fallen into such a train. The blood rushed to her pale cheeks, for to her it was a species of disloyalty to Noel to have had these thoughts. She had such confidence in him, born of her deep and unselfish love for the man.

But there was no need for her to beautify herself. He had never noticed her gowns, never spoken of their becomingness or their lack of it. She knew how absolutely and completely her heart belonged to him. He must have been blind, indeed, not to be able to read those great, clear, calm grey eyes — so full of tenderness, so very beautiful and soulful when their long dark lashes shut out the greener light of day and gave the glow of her soul a chance to be seen and felt!

No, she would not beautify her person any more than had been her wont. It would be to admit a lack of confidence in herself — more than that, a lack of confidence in Noel! But she would leave nothing undone to please him: nothing which a thoughtful and considerate fiancée should do. Hence she began to devote herself most assiduously to her music. She practised the songs he admired, learned new ones, and was specially careful to provide herself with a number of duets, so that they might sing together. To Caroline song was far more than it was to the ordinary worldly woman, and when Noel's full, deep, resonant voice chorded with hers it seemed to her a proof that their lives would melt into a harmony as their voices did.

But she thought of other things, too; things not quite so poetic and ethereal. Her tennis, for instance, and set to improve her game; for he played, and — in private, again — in that favourite corridor retreat of hers, in fact — she read through the whole accumulation of his letters, from the very beginning of the engagement. This romantic task occupied her from morning till night — the night of his arrival. It was long since she had looked at the earlier letters; and they pleased her. They were not so sensible as late ones, by any means, but they were rather more flattering, and indeed they had come oftener than twice a week in those days. Caroline lingered over these old letters, and though those of the last years were wise and witty and kind, the former appealed most strongly to her present mood. The leaves whispered to her as she read and dreamed; the birds sang all around her; for this haunt of hers was merely a little clearing among the trees, where rotted a worm-eaten table and garden seat. And on the latter next morning Noel and she sat together — at opposite ends of it — in the most sensible manner imaginable.

Their conversation also showed their sense.

"It is a charming spot," said Rev. Noel Pennyman (certainly they had been sitting there some time); "it really is."

"I am glad you like it. I love it!" Caroline added a little shyly — "And you know why?"

"Why?" asked Mr Pennyman, innocently.

"Because — because it was here that you — "

"Ah! I remember! May one smoke in it, Car? That I forgot."

"Of course you may," said Caroline, hurt at his asking.

It took him some moments to fill his pipe and some more artfully to light it. The performance claimed his undivided attention. And Caroline watched him, from under her expansive sun-hat. He was a handsome, soldierly fellow, with fine features, dark eyes, and a moustache. Sitting here in flannels, lighting his pipe, he suggested any type rather than that of the British curate, which he represented. Yet he was decently grave, and in point of fact a sufficiently zealous and earnest young priest. He was as ardent and idealistic as ever about his work; as Caroline had found out from the most fluent talk they had yet had, which had been on this subject. In other directions he was less eloquent, less enthusiastic, than of old, and Caroline was hurt at more than his asking leave to smoke and pretending to forget that it was here he had proposed to her.

"I remember," added Caroline, after a pause that broke the point of the remark, "that you used not to ask permission to smoke, last time you were here."

"Ah, last time I was here."

"It's ages ago, isn't it?" She produced a smile.

He mentioned the number of months, which we know. His pipe was behaving beautifully.

"I hope it will never be so long again!" exclaimed Caroline, impulsively.

He regarded her reflectively from the other end of the seat. There was a look of pain in his eyes which she saw and remembered. Then they grew kind.

"My dear girl," said Pennyman, half in rebuke, half in regret, "you know exactly how it has been. The length of England is between us, and last year when I took my holiday I was obliged to go to my mother — we nearly lost her. As long as I am up there I don't see how we can meet oftener than once a year, but then very likely I shan't be there another year; surely I may begin now to hope for a living! And I shall get one, you'll see; and it shall come right in the end!"

He said it kindly, though not, perhaps, in the voice of conviction. But Caroline was very much moved.

"Will it?" she cried, peering pensively into his eyes. "Will it?"

His face filled with pity and compassion. "God grant it may!" he hoarsely whispered, and he kissed her forehead once.

"'I will give my life to you, Caroline!'" She never forgot how he said this.

And the days of Pennyman's visit passed on very pleasantly, on the whole, and on the surface. The interesting pair were a good deal together — entirely together — yet not so much as had been anticipated; indeed, they proved a singularly unobjectionable pair in this and similar respects; they were sensible to a degree. Noel moreover made himself extremely agreeable to the younger girls — escorted them round the countryside, played hard sets with them and sang charmingly in the school-room. If they caught him sometimes looking worried and perplexed — as more than once one or other of them did — they put it down to the shortness of his holiday and the uncertainty of his and Caroline's future. The same applied to Caroline, who was perceived (in the school-room) to be getting rather glum. This was odd, certainly, with Noel in the house; but naturally she wished to be married, and now that he was here today, and practically gone tomorrow, most likely for another year, the engagement might well seem interminable. That there could be any other ground for unhappiness never entered those pretty, frivolous heads in the school-room; that there was something wrong somewhere — something delicate and deep and vital — they were incapable of suspecting. The two were continually together; that was enough for the girls. If they were not happy it was their own fault, they ought to be; the younger Miss Teagues had no sympathy with people who made themselves unhappy. But the younger Miss Teagues were not keen observers, either, or toward the end of the week they must have noticed in Caroline signs of too little sleep, which even the rector observed, though he held his tongue.

On the Sunday evening Pennyman had promised to preach. He was shut up for hours on Saturday writing his sermon and secretly glad to be able to seclude himself. While he was busy

Miss Teague took the opportunity of visiting some of her people, who, of course, knew perfectly well who was staying at the rectory. She does not seem to have struck her folk as being particularly jubilant, "considering". And to those who asked her, as no doubt they all did, when it was to be, she appears to have answered, in a manner variously described:

"I may never be married at all!"

Certainly the engagement had dragged on for a very long time.

On her return to the rectory, however, Caroline Teague sought Noel Pennyman, her betrothed, and was with him when he finished his sermon. She rose and bent over his shoulder as he flung down his pen, and asked, wistfully enough, if she might look, but Pennyman pushed his manuscript aside.

"No, Car," said he, without turning his head; "I'd rather you didn't look, if you don't mind!"

"Then won't you read it to me?" she could not help pleading; though she had coloured up behind his back.

"You will hear it all tomorrow, my dear girl."

"Ah, I am looking forward to that; only — only I should have liked to hear a little of it now!"

"Don't ask me, Car," he answered, never looking at her. "What's the good of your hearing it twice? Besides, you wouldn't like it, really you wouldn't."

"You might leave me to be the judge of that," said Caroline, gently. "As to the good of it, I don't say there would be any. Yet you used to say I should have a little voice in all your sermons one day!"

"Do let us be sensible!" exclaimed Pennyman, and that frayed and chafed her.

His elbows were on the writing table, his hands supported his head. She was still standing behind his chair; so he never knew of her tears. There was merely a pause. She was calm

81

— she might have been smiling — when she enquired if it was a very deep theological discourse.

"There is very little theology in it, I am afraid," said he; "it is about — "

"Well?"

"About doing one's duty," said Pennyman, with a kind of groan.

"Well, that covers everything, and applies to us all!"

"To us all!" he repeated bitterly.

A light hand had lain for a moment on his shoulder; it lay there another moment rather heavily. "Noel!" she murmured. He felt her breath upon his cheek; but nothing more; she left him abruptly, without finishing her sentence — without beginning it, indeed.

On the Monday Pennyman was going to Oxford — a Sabbath day's journey from Rix — to look up some old friends there. He was to stay half the week, returning to the rectory to finish his holiday and to preach another sermon for Mr Teague. He preached the first with such effect that the congregation kept awake to listen — a compliment they paid old Mr Teague only on the coldest Sundays in winter. The personality of the young clergyman was striking and his method anti-narcotic and new to Rix, I am afraid; but he had a special interest in the eyes of the parishioners as the betrothed of their beloved young lady. The church was quite exceptionally crowded; and after the sermon it was admitted — on the strict hypothesis that any mere man could be in the least worthy of that angel — that this handsome young divine, with the pale face and earnest voice, would be hard to beat for the place.

He was certainly very pale tonight; and his voice was peculiarly earnest. The lights were lowered in the old church when the young man knelt in the pulpit, and the hymn was over, and Miss Teague, in the organ loft, had driven home the stops. The four evangelists on the chancel window were half faded against the summer evening sky; the church was filled with a bluish dusk — stabbed at the pulpit by the flames of four candles, which shone downward on the preacher's papers and upward into his face. He was, indeed, very pale; and Caroline, intently watching him from the loft, heard every word of that sermon which was the turning point of her life and his. It was about doing one's duty, as he had said; and the well-worn theme was not treated with any striking degree of originality. But the preacher was in striking earnest, though he did read his lines. He seemed to feel personally and acutely every sentence he uttered; and when he introduced as only curates can the inevitable quotation from the modern poet (parishioners thought it was Pennyman's own), he seemed to feel that, too — this!

His honour rooted in dishonour stood,
And faith unfaithful kept him falsely true.

He was speaking, you understand, of the difficulties of duty, the two-edged difficulties, and so on; and he was speaking just then in ringing, tremulous tones. He worked in the Tennyson quite naturally, though God knows why he worked it in at all, unless he thought of this way. But he had never spoken so sincerely, so strenuously, in his life; and parishioners envied his congregation in the north of England, where they actually supposed he spoke like this every Sunday of his life!

Miss Teague played the people out of the church, walked home with Pennyman and her father (who would talk of nothing but the sermon and congratulated them both on it), sat through the usual Sunday supper — an elaborate and animated meal at the rectory — was entirely her amiable, unselfish self until she went to bed, which happened early. She did not kiss Noel when she said good night to him; but the others were there, and it was notorious how sensible Noel and she were on such points. She did, however, give him a kind smile and a generous hand, though now she knew that he loved her no longer and had not the moral courage to tell her so plainly.

She fought it all out in her room that night. On the very evening of his arrival, in their first talk together — nay, in the first glance he had given her — she had missed something; and now she knew what. He had been kind and good, even gentle, with all his coolness, but he loved her then no longer; had he ever really loved her at all? She looked once more at his earliest letters. And, well, if he had not loved her then, he had cheated and worked himself into a counterfeit passion, which at least had all the warmth of the sacred flame. This is what I say; but Caroline kissed those early letters and blotted them with her tears. The later ones dried her eyes, though they powerfully supported her present conviction; they were too clever and logical and far too sensible for love letters; as his conduct had been far too sensible for that of a lover all this week, their first together for eighteen months. And tonight he had exposed his whole weak soul to her in a sermon! But did he guess that she had translated him? Would he do his duty yet? Did he know his duty? She remembered — she would never forget — how he had said, under the trees, the other morning, "I will give my life to you, Caroline." She did not want his life. She wanted his love. Next to the knowledge that he loved her she would have had his own brave, voluntary confession that he did not love her. She would have given everything that night — everything still — to have admired, as she had admired him, the man she had loved — the soul she must love for forever.

84

In the dead of night and in the silver of the sunny morning — motionless on her knees and rocking to and fro in her chair — Caroline Teague wrestled with her grief as best she might, placing her humble spirit in the hands of him to whom she walked so near. And the following forenoon she accompanied Noel Pennyman through the sunny fields to the station and came back in haste.

She found the rector in his study at his desk.

"Father," she murmured, "I have seen him off!"

The rector did not raise his eyes. "Well, my dear, he'll be back in a couple of days," he remarked cheerfully, his nose in his papers.

"No; he is never coming at all!"

The rector raised his head, pushed up his spectacles and gazed at his daughter in dire amazement.

"What!" he gasped, "has there been a quarrel?

"No — no quarrel."

"What then, Caroline, in heaven's name?"

"I have given him up," said Caroline, firmly.

Mr Teague sprang up.

"You have jilted him — Noel Pennyman — the man you have been engaged to all these years?"

"I have jilted him."

The rector made her repeat it more than once. "May I ask why?" he enquired at length.

"Because — " Caroline hesitated — "because — you can't marry without love on both sides. This has been a cruel, a wicked mistake from the very beginning. Thank God I have discovered it in time!"

"You mean for your discovery that you do not care for him?" cried the rector sharply — more sharply than he had spoken to her in all his life.

Caroline bowed her head. "Yes, I meant that!"

Mr Teague sat down at his desk and leaned heavily on his hand. "I am ashamed of you, Caroline," he said in a broken voice. "I am ashamed of my daughter."

But now Miss Teague could bear no more; she fell upon her knees at his feet and burst into passionate tears. All that she now said was reiterated many times; and much of it was incoherent.

"Oh, do not be hard on me. I have no one left, but you. I will help you as it has been my delight and pride always to help you; so will I help you to the end. My happiness made no difference to my work, did it? My unhappiness shall make no difference, either. Rather, it is better than if he had given me up, isn't it? The world is more lenient, I am sure — in this one thing — to the woman than to the man. And you will be less hard on me, won't you, than you would have been on him? Forgive me, father! I have only you."

The rector laid his trembling hand upon her hair.

"Get up, my darling! I am not your judge. May he forgive you — and may God! Yet Caroline, Caroline! I had rather it were the young man who had done this thing — not my daughter!"

Miss Teague arose and went away drooping; for now, indeed, her heart seemed broken. She went to that little place, her favourite place, where Noel had proposed to her — where Noel had seemed vexed at being reminded of that proposal — where she had opened her letters. Here, also, she buried all that; and set her spirit toward what was to be.

Now the Rev. Noel Pennyman, saved by this strong soul from a humiliating duty — which it is still but fair to believe he might have performed in the end — has never appreciated Miss Teague's magnanimity. For she vowed she did not love him, and though, in doing so, she snatched similar words from his mouth, and relieved his soul, his vanity carries the scar to this day. She loved him, in fine, so well that she managed in that walk to the station to convince him that she did not love him at all. So his friends in the North, and even Miss Teague's friends, consider that poor Mr Pennyman was treated abominably. And who are we to disagree with their verdict?

The Romance of Sergeant Clancy

Miss Slagg was asleep. He toes pointed placidly to the cloudless blue, a pine-trunk propped her shoulders; the intervening frock was of obsolete fashion and extreme shabbiness, and was crowned by a very old, very big wideawake, below which were visible the point of Miss Slagg's chin, an ear reddened through by the sun, and some strands of dark hair similarly tinged. No more than a mile westward, the same rays heatened to crackling point the galvanized roofings of Cockatoo Corner, and within half that distance lay the river-timber. Miss Slagg, however, finding herself nearing home earlier than usual, was not keen to arrive, nor yet to tempt the river-timber, an occasional haunt of her father's at this hour. Here where she was she had decided to "camp"; and here she slept, while the shadows lengthened and the crows drew round to cock their heads and watch. Two dead rabbits, at the sleeper's side, allured the crows: no other creatures saw her until the new police-sergeant came driving by, in plain clothes, and descried her from the road.

Now Sergeant Clancy, the new man at Cockatoo Corner, was, in his way, a special person; he was quite different from the ordinary mounted constable of the Colonies. His speciality was an imagination of his own. This imagination was of the restless kind which would have proved a distinct advantage in the detective department down in Sydney; but in the back-blocks it was no advantage at all. The Sergeant's own imagination he fed in his leisure on that of other imaginative men, the novelists; and as his leisure had been large, so was the flavour of romance about him strong and stale. He was new to Corner, so new as now to be returning from the station with his very first supply of mutton; he was still examining the township through romantic glasses, as the potential scene of the kind of things he read of but never had a chance of doing. And the sight of Miss Slagg among the pines more nearly hinted at such a thing than anything he had seen or heard of yet. For instance, she might not be asleep at all, but dead. This obviously was not the case, but the Sergeant pulled up, jumped down, and drew near to inspect.

He saw before him a spectacle in which there was little to attract; for the clothes were ragged, the boots in holes, the hands large, and the face invisible. He did not know it was Miss Slagg; indeed, he knew the Slaggs by reputation only, and this since his visit to the station this afternoon. But it was a woman: the gallant Sergeant looked instinctively for the attendant peril for which fiction had taught him to yearn. There was none. There was no snake in the sand crawling on to attack, no savage waving his boomerang behind the tree. There was no first-class danger to rescue her from. But the woman's wideawake was tilted so far forward that part of her head was exposed to the sun; and this seemed to constitute a danger of the second class. The Sergeant tugged up half a blue-bush, and stole forward to adjust it behind the unconscious head, remembering as he did so that he had read something of the kind once in a story.

"Be off to blazes!"

The words cracked out distinct, harsh, and separate, as a revolver spits, and they shot Clancy two yards backward, shrub in hand. They came from under the wideawake, which was raised a little by one of the large, sunburnt hands, so that the Sergeant now beheld the full lips and even teeth from which the words had been fired.

"Excuse me," he stammered, " but sunstroke — "

"You an' your sunstroke!"

The wideawake was pushed higher still. Clancy saw half the face now, and was attracted.

"I wished to protect you from the sun," he protested, with perhaps conscious gallantry — "that was all; I never meant to disturb you."

She eyed him from the ground. He was not a very fine fellow to look at. He was thin and tall, and he stooped; his face was sallow, he wore a short black beard, and his mahogany hands had a fleshless look, the muscles knotting over them like the roots of a tree from which the soil has drifted.

"Well," said Miss Slagg, "who *are* you, anyway?"

"My name's Clancy."

"The new Sergeant?"

"Yes."

"Well, I'll be bothered!" exclaimed Miss Slagg, sitting bolt upright, and opening her dark eyes wide. "I've seen you across the road, in uniform, but I'm blessed if I'd ha' tumbled to you as you are! The barracks is right opposite our shanty — me and father's. I'm Nancy Slagg, d'ye see? Nancy and Sergeant Clancy — that's a rhyme! Likely you've heard of us?"

"Yes, I've heard of you," said Clancy, pleasantly: he had never taken his eyes from hers since those striking orbs had become visible.

"Very bad?" inquired the girl.

"Never mind; I don't believe all I hear; I take people as I find 'em. And I don't go poking my nose into what's no concern o' mine; you can ask 'em where I come from; and I don't mind who you tell that I said so, Miss Nancy Slagg. You can tell them that may like to know, that the new bobby minds his own business as a rule. And now, if you're going that way, I'll give you a lift back to the township — most happy!" added the Sergeant rather grandly, suddenly remembering his favourite literature, which he had temporarily forgotten.

"No, thanks," replied Nancy, decidedly.

"Why not?"

"Because I'll walk."

She sprang up as she spoke, but immediately reeled back to the tree: one foot she could not put to the ground.

"You've sprained your ankle!" cried the Sergeant, finding himself, to his delight, in one of the familiar heroic situations after all. "You *must* let me give you a lift now. I insist on helping you into my trap — stop, I'll bring it up to you!" And the gallant fellow was running to do so when her laugh arrested him.

"Not sprained!" said she, kicking out her right foot. "Asleep!"

The Sergeant was disappointed.

"I don't know whether to believe you or not. Why shouldn't I drive you, though? Your place and mine too are right at this end of the township."

"Shall I tell you?"

"Yes."

"Get aboard then - 'cause I'm *not* coming."

He did so reluctantly. "Now, then," said he, "tell me what makes you so stubborn!"

Nancy Slagg had whipped off her wideawake, and was swinging it in one hand, while the other knuckled her side, showing to shapely advantage the strong arm and elbow in the shabby old sleeve. Her dark hair, half up, half down, glowed in the sun as before afire: so did her eyes: so did her whole face, from the forehead, where the sunburn began, to her throat, where it ended in a collar of white skin conspicuous whenever she raised her head. She raised it now, in her uncouth

91

coquetry, and gave the Sergeant a broad grin, and a thrill to treasure in his sentimental soul.

"First of all I don't want: second of all, if I did, the old man he'd — "

"What?   He ill-treats you, I've heard so today," cried Clancy, in some excitement: "but you don't mean to say that just for — "

"I don't mean to say not another word.   Whoever's been telling you is a bloomin' liar, and you can say so from me — and tell him to mind his own bloomin' business!   I'd say the same thing to you, Sergeant, if you hadn't told me you minded yours of your own accord.   And I believe you.   See?" Her eyes had flashed; but now she was grinning again.

"I see," said the Sergeant, discreetly.

"So long, then."

"So long."   And with yet greater discretion, foreign to his habit, the inspired Sergeant drove off at once, without another word, though not without another look.   He glanced back presently along the wide, sandy track; and Miss Slagg was trudging after him with long, unfeminine steps, swinging a dead rabbit in either hand.

From that day forward, Sergeant Clancy inhaled the atmosphere of personal romance for which he had long pined. Here was a wild but glorious girl living at the mercy of a wretch of a father.   They inhabited a hovel; no one trusted them; the father was an inveterate villain; the girl a lovely, unfriended savage — until the Sergeant's advent.   He befriended her, and more.   He loved her from the first.   It was the romance of his life, for which he had waited patiently.

The villainous Slagg was one of those picturesque persons who decorate the outer rings of civilisation more often than the populous bull's eye.   He was of the medium height and build, had really handsome features (when newly shaved), and he had

92

given Nancy her eyes. But he was the acknowledged rogue of the district, and the Sergeant smoked an occasional evening pipe with him at the peril of his own position. He ran the risk sometimes, however, and when he did Nancy would be there. More often he would manage to encounter her when going the round of her rabbit-traps, and the girl would laugh and fling slang at him across a gulf of her own fixing, captivating him in her own way. It was a way that strengthened without tightening existing bonds. She encouraged him in her rough fashion, yet kept him at a disheartening distance, and this with a facility really astonishing in one so purely a child of nature. It never occurred to him that the encouragement was not genuine, but enforced by old Slagg, who would score considerably by an attachment between his daughter and the Sergeant, through the latter's consequent attitude towards himself.

Slagg had a reputation for sheep-stealing: he had been caught at it, and convicted, before this; and it was Clancy's dread that it might fall to him to catch and convict the old sinner again. I am afraid the gallant Sergeant neglected his severest duty for the sake of Slagg's daughter and her brilliant eyes; either there were some things he would not see, or he was blind and unfit for the force. What he saw with all his soul, and naturally to the eclipse of duty, was the uncouth beauty of this strapping girl; and later, her good heart. For she had merits other than her eyes and hair, the ripe tint of her skin, or the graceful curves which old clothes, never made for Nancy, could not hide. Of the two inhabitants of the hovel opposite the police-barracks, it was the girl who supplied the necessaries of their lives — always barring the mutton, which was a luxury, and never paid for. Nancy was the rabbiter, who went the round of her traps every day, and carried the skins to the station once a week, where they fetched sixpence each. Nancy had paid for the piebald pony which her father rode, and from which he had fallen more than once when in drink. Nancy carved the emu-eggs, and carved them better than anyone else in those parts, so that her work would have paid her really well had she known its actual value. And it was Nancy who took care of her disreputable old father, drunk or sober, and bore his violence in either state, brooking no word against him from sympathising neighbours.

Past Cockatoo Corner, and immediately behind the tenement of old Slagg, flowed one of the rivers which gave to this part of New South Wales the name of the Riverina; that is to say, it so flowed three seasons out of four: in summer it became a mere chain of waterholes. Though the surrounding country was free from forest, the river banks were well timbered, and behind the hovel the savage Nancy could boast of that luxury of civilised girlhood — a favourite tree. The tree was a willow with a fork jutting over the river. In this fork Nancy Slagg would sit carving, occasionally, in the afternoon: or dreaming, more often, of an evening. Of those dreams she could have told you little: only that it was strange to sit perched between two starry skies, midway, in a single belt of whispering timber: always strange, sometimes sickly; for she could have told you what it was to sit there too long, until the stars spun round overhead and underneath, and what an age it took to creep back along the trunk with tight-shut eyes and chattering teeth.

But once, when it was merely strange, a black figure punted a primitive raft round the bend near the township — seeming to shoot right out of the trees — and passed clean under the forked willow.

"Who is it?" cried Nancy, startled out of her shapeless dreams.

"Hyslop," responded a young man, who, indeed, was equally startled.

"Never heard of him! Who are you?"

"The new hand at Gulland's store."

The young man grasped the branches and lifted his face ; and Nancy, peering through them, found it to her liking. He had made his raft in an hour of empty solitude; he improved, strengthened and elaborated it later with pains and ecstasy. And under the forked willow, behind Slagg's hut, the raft lay hidden most evenings when the moon was not perilously bright.

It did not last long. One dark night, well within the month, the hunter suddenly discovered that he had overshot the place. Then a block of wood whizzed past his head and splashed into the water near the further bank; and, looking round, our young man saw that the willow of delight had been hewn down, and made out the form of old Slagg seated on the stump. A volley of oaths, thickly uttered, followed the missle; but Hylop, a good specimen of the cool Australian youth, had the presence of mind to punt on; and old Slagg, being drunk, took another lump of wood from the ground and waited patiently for the enemy's return passage. And while he waited, young Hyslop, who had landed higher up, was quietly interviewing Miss Slagg in the hovel itself, and undertaking to avenge at convenience a certain ugly blue mark upon her wrist.

Luckily for everybody (excepting, perhaps the common hangman), they were not caught.

Slagg sought the Sergeant next day and bluntly asked him if he meant to let this whipper- snapper of a counter-jumper snatch the girl from under his very nose. The Sergeant had made few friends in the township; he had not so much as heard of young Hyslop, and he was fairly astounded to hear of his audacity and Nancy's crimes. Slagg left him in the state of mind he had desired to induce. He did not mean to lose his girl to Clancy either; but that was for future prevention. Clancy would be useful meanwhile. Slagg crossed the road, chuckling, and gave his daughter a delicate reminder of his authority and power by taking from her the emu-egg which she was busily carving, and stamping it into pieces with his heel.

Meanwhile the Sergeant endured all she torments of the losing lover. He had not yet literally lost; but, as he reflected, there was little to choose between the girl who had not said "No" — because she had not been asked — and the girl who held clandestine meetings with some other man. He was as miserable as he could have been had she refused him for the hundredth time. And in his misery he went to Gulland's store, to purchase an article he did not want, and to take stock of the man who had undermined him. The latter betrayed no embarrassment; he was a cool hand, as we have seen, even for a young Colonial; he talked of the roads and the state of the roads with perfect ease, and some little civility. He turned out to be a young fellow of medium build and height, with decided features, and a great air of independence, which Nancy was the very girl — reflected the Sergeant sadly — to admire in a man. Clancy, indeed, was much more dispirited than incensed by the sight of his rival. For the sterner feeling he had no time, this was filled with involuntary reflection upon his own inferiority, from a young woman's point of view. On leaving the store he made a casual inquiry or two respecting the new assistant there; and these served only to deepen his dejection; for already the young man seemed to bear an excellent character in the township.

Before the day was over Clancy encountered the young man again; this time unintentionally. It was late in the evening, near the pine-ridge where he had first set eyes on Nancy Slagg and whither he now wandered — egregiously enough — to calm his soul. And the young man was not alone; Nancy Slagg was with him.

The Sergeant strode back to the township, breathing hard, and met old Slagg on his way out.

"Have you seen my girl Nancy?" asked Slagg, excitedly.

The Sergeant had no time to consider. He let his instinct answer, and astonished himself by saying steadily: "No — I haven't."

"They're together somewhere — damn them!"

"Are you sure?"

"Pretty positive; and I thought it was somewhere in this direction; but — you've not seen a trace of 'em, eh?"

"Not a trace," answered the Sergeant, already half regretting his instinctive lie, and wholly marvelling at it, but sticking to it as one does to a lie once told.

So Slagg was thrown off that particular scent, and whatever happened later in the hovel there was no collision between Hyslop and the old man that night, nor the next, nor the night after that. Then came a darker one than usual, and what was rarer, a gentle rain.

The Sergeant sat in his verandah, thinking, to the rather agreeable accompaniment of raindrops on a corrugated iron roof. He was also smoking, and his spirit was comparatively calm. Affairs, too, had calmed somewhat during the last three days. The youth Hyslop was conducting himself as admirably as ever behind his counter, and was but seldom seen outside the premises; in fact, he was running no more risks. Moreover, some sort of reconciliation seemed to have taken place between the two Slaggs. And above all, Nancy had been civil — more than civil for Nancy Slagg — to Sergeant Clancy. So the good Sergeant was once more smoking the pipe of peace not in name only. His imagination was itself again, and the picture of Nancy, becomingly dressed, and enthroned in this very verandah as his wife — this picture, which had got out of focus, was now as clearly defined as it had ever been.

97

He was considering ways of strengthening his hand. One way he had thought of in the beginning of things, when all his ideas had come from books, and this among them. It was to detect and incarcerate the old sheep-stealer — that were not hard — and to convert him, in durance vile, into the ace of trumps. The girl, in her way, was devoted to her father. The ingenuous Sergeant did not, indeed, propose to hold a pistol to this devotion. But if he allowed himself to be prevailed upon, and, at the last, and most dramatic moment, set the father free, the effect on the girl might be as that of the pistol, with a less disagreeable after-effect. His sense of official duty had become regrettably demoralised, partly owing (no doubt) to an unhealthy appetite for fiction.

But Sergeant Clancy read books as he would have eaten fancy puddings without inquiring, even in his own mind, how they were made. So he did not see very clearly his way through the situation suggested. It kept him up very late indeed, and then something happened to keep him up all night. Something real: a horseman rode out from behind the shanty of old Slagg, and passed close to the barracks, heading in the direction of Cockatoo Station. It was still raining, it was darker than ever, but the piebald pony was unmistakable as it passed the angle of the barracks; and if that were not old Slagg astride of her, Sergeant Clancy, as he buckled on the belt that supported his revolver, desired himself to be shot. The old man was after no good; he would follow, and discover what bad; and as to the end — it depended.

Two hours later he was back in the verandah — at one end of it — wet through with rain and sweat; crouching, with his revolver in one hand and the other hollowed at his ear. Hoof-sounds met it: the thief was returning with his plunder: and it was not sheep, but horses!

At this end of the township the sand was heavy; none should know it better than old Slagg; and Clancy was not surprised when the two driven horses trotted close by the barracks — close to where he knelt — their hoofs effectually muffled in the deep sand. But as the piebald passed the Sergeant leapt out, and pulled the rider to the ground. The man seemed dazed. The revolver, too, cowed him. He pulled the wideawake further down over his eyes — as if Clancy did not know him! He submitted to be pushed along the verandah, and into the strong room, without a word, and without a single motion of resistance, though the muscles of his arms, as Clancy gripped them, were firm and hard as those of a young man. Neither did Clancy speak; the thing was done in tragic silence, and in a matter of seconds. The cell door banged, the key grated in the lock, and after that Sergeant Clancy leant against a verandah-post, and heard nothing but his own heart beating.

Half that he had plotted then was now a living fact; but he did not think of that, he was far enough from plots and stories in the midst of the most striking reality of his life. His brain was bewildered by the events embedding it; he pressed his head to the post, leaned hard on it, and closed his eyes.

When he opened them another face was close to his in the darkness — the face of Nancy Slagg.

"What'll he get?" she whispered, hoarsely.

"Get?" said Clancy, for it did not clarify his understanding to see her there, and face her now. "What will *who* get?"

Nancy pointed to where the small barred window was: the window itself was invisible in the dense darkness of the verandah.

"Him!"

"Oh, him. Nancy, I'm so sorry!"

"What'll he get?"

"God knows!"

He was looking down upon her very sorrowfully, very tenderly. The girl met his look, and read it.

"I say, Sergeant! S'pose you ain't to be got at — eh?"

"No! How can you ask!"

"'Cause there's nothin' I wouldn't do for you, Sergeant, to let him go — nothin'! You've been good to me all along."

The Sergeant trembled.   "Do you mean it, Nancy?" he whispered, brokenly. "Do you mean it?"

"What'll he get?" asked the girl once more, dropping back into her first words and tone.

"A long time — a long time!"

"Long or short, it'd ruin him for life," said Nancy bitterly; and her head drooped, her fingers wrenched one another, as she made up her mind.   "Yes, I do mean it!" she cried, looking him squarely in the face. "*I* mean it — do you?   *Will* you let him go? It's no good makin' any bloomin' bones about it. I mean — if you wanted me to-— I'd marry you!"

"He's free," said the Sergeant, very distinctly.   Then, with a single sob, he caught her in his arms and to his breast, and she did not immediately resist; it was a part of the bargain.   Long moments to each of them — of hell to her, of heaven to him — moments that both might carry to their death — he held her tight.   At last she released herself, quietly, and looked up at him with so white a face that he heard again the rattle of the rain that had never ceased.   Then Nancy spoke, and her words were the words of mystery.

"There was no other way, and he's been a great brute to me always, has the old man, but never such a brute as over this. He'd have killed my Jack — and he tried   So we said next time he got tight we would do a bolt — and he's been paralytic tight since sundown. But we couldn't bolt on our legs, 'cause he'd have had me back in the morning. The other evening — time you saw us — I'd been with my Jack to the horse-paddock, and I shown him them two horses you've got there, 'cause they wouldn't miss 'em first thing in the mornin' like they'd miss station horses. What's up? Didn't you know they was yours? Why, they loafed straight into your yard by theirselves; but you was here."

From a state of entire mystification, Clancy had passed, during this explanation, to one of incredulity.

"Nancy," he cried, weakly smiling, as at chaff, "your father's sober enough tonight; it's your father I've run in"

"I wish it *was* my father, it's my Jack!"

The Sergeant remembered the dense darkness (it grew lighter as they talked), the wideawake pulled forward, and the firm muscles for old arms.

"Hyslop!" he said, with a gasp. "Hyslop, I suppose!"

"Yes, Jack Hyslop — my Jack. That's why I'm going to do what I've promised you I'll do — to set my Jack scot free!"

She seemed to speak of what she could not realise, for her fine eyes were dry, and dull; but she spoke on one hard despairing note that struck straighter to the heart than tears.

"Your Jack! Then you love him — all this much?"

"You may have me if you let him go. My poor old Jack! You'd be done for, like father, when you came out!"

In the lessening darkness the Sergeant looked into her dull, sad eyes; and life rolled out before him, with those splendid eyes always his, dull and sad to the end. And that was enough. He stepped inside, and came back with a key, which he put in Nancy's hands. "Let him out yourself," he said. "God knows what I have been thinking of doing!"

He went round to the yard, and bridled the two horses he found there; for they were his own. He led them out in the rain, and in the darkness, which was not the darkness that had been.

He regretted the growing light, for in it Nancy Slagg and Jack Hyslop took well-nigh a furlong to vanish, the two together, riding away for ever from Cockatoo Corner. And it had been bad enough to be left standing in eternal darkness, with Nancy's wild, impetuous kiss red-hot on his cheek, and her tears of gratitude still wet upon his face.

But daylight found Sergeant Clancy kneeling at the tree where he had seen her first, and stripping off the bark, just where her head had rested. He had become alive to the fact that his personal love story had reared suddenly, and toppled over without his knowing it. He was now performing the kind of final act his reading taught him to expect of himself, as the hero of his own romance.

The Crimean Shirt

It is now rather more than twelve years since the disappearance and the finding of Henry Powell, on Mooroolooloo Station, New South Wales, and rather less than the subsequent case in which I myself was perhaps the principal witness. And I think that the time has arrived for confessing that the evidence which I gave on that occasion, though, indeed, "nothing but the truth", was nevertheless not "the whole truth" at all.

I did not and I do not believe there was a single being in that colonial Court who would have credited the whole truth had I told it there and then upon my oath. Nor was it essential to the case. Nor did I care to return to the station, new chum as I still was, with yet another handle for native-born buffoonery. But I am no longer the store-keeper of Mooroolooloo; and I believe the public mind to be broader than it was in the matter of so-called ghosts. At all events, I am going to tell you for the first time what my own eyes saw, on a day and night in January, in the year 1884. I had been some six weeks in the Riverina, and I was alone at our home-station for the night. The owner was paying us a visit. He and the manager were camping at an outstation nineteen miles away. The overseer was absent on his holiday. I had the homestead to myself, for there was neither woman nor child upon the place. Suddenly, between nine and ten o'clock, as I sat smoking and thinking on the back verandah, a spur jingled, and I made out the crinkled moleskins and the felt wideawake of one of the men.

"Powell, the rabbiter, is lost in the bush, mister," said he.

I sprang to my feet, for the news was like that of a man overboard at sea.

"How long has he been out?"

"Since yesterday morning."

"But I thought he camped with old Wylie at the Five-mile whim?"

"So he does."

"Then why didn't Wylie come in sooner?"

"Ah! there you hit it," said my man. "That's what we've all been asking him, but Wylie says his mate was given to stopping odd nights at other chaps' camps, and he never thought anything of it till he didn't turn up this evening. Even if he had, he couldn't have left the whim, Wylie couldn't with no other water anywhere near, and the sheep drawing to the troughs from four paddocks. But he's come in now, and he's up at the hut if you like to see him." And at the men's hut I found the whim-driver, the centre still of an attentive group, but no longer, I thought, the target of questions and cross-questions implying criticism and blame. On the contrary, there was now every token of sympathy with the anxiety and distress of mind from which Wylie was obviously suffering, and at the sight of which I also could spare him some of the pity which I felt for the missing rabbiter. The whim-driver was an elderly man, with brown wrinkles all over his face, and grey whiskers parting at a baggy throat; but he was still powerfully built, and a typical bushman with his eagle eye and his strong bare arms. His eye, however, was hot with horror and, remorse as it met mine, and the whole man twitched as he told me his tale.

"If only I had guessed anything was wrong, Mr Forrester," he cried, "I would have left the sheep in a minute, though my billet depended upon it. But he's so often stopped away one night that it never bothered me till the day wore on and he didn't come back. God forgive me, I never even thought of telling the bosses when they passed this morning on their way to the out-station. Yet I might ha' known — I might ha' known! He was a sailor, poor Powell was, and sailors are

104

always the worst bushmen. I've known him get bushed before, but only for an hour or two. And to think of him being out all this time — in this heat, with not a drop of water in the crab-holes! He may — he may be dead already — my poor mate, my poor mate!"

With that he turned his back upon us, in the most evident agitation, so that we thought it kindest not to refer to him in the brief council of war which the men and I now held together. It was promptly decided that all hands should form a search party to start at daybreak, with the exception of Wylie and myself. Wylie must return to his troughs. My knowledge of the country was as yet very limited, and therefore I was the one who could best be spared to ride at once to the out-station, and inform the 'bosses' of what had occurred. The night-horse was the only animal in the yard, but I took it to save time, and shortly after ten o'clock rode off with Wylie, our way coinciding as far as the whim.

There was no moon, and the night was anything but clear for that load of bright stars and cloudless skies. A hot north wind of several days' duration had flown suddenly into the south, whence it was now blowing hard and chill, so that I buttoned my coat up as we cantered side by side, and took off my eye-glasses lest the rushing wind should lift them from my nose. We spoke very little as we rode, though once more, when we drew rein and ambled for a little, my companion reproached himself for not having given an earlier alarm.

It was impossible not to feel sorry for him, but equally impossible to acquit him of blame, so I said very little in reply. When we came to the hut a dull red glow burnt steadily within, and Wylie sighed bitterly as he explained that he had built up the fire before leaving, that his poor mate might find all comfortable if some happy chance should bring him back. He added that he supposed I would push straight on without dismounting; but I was cold and the glow looked graceful and I had slipped from the saddle before the words were out of his mouth. Next moment I uttered a loud cry.

Tho door of the hut was at one end, to the left of the dying fire, and at the opposite end were two low, rude bunks, one in each corner. On the foot of the right-hand bunk sat a figure I could have sworn to even without my glasses. It was the missing rabbiter, in a red-checked suit which I had often seen him wear, and his face was buried in his hands.

"Wylie," cried I, wheeling round on the threshold, "he has come back, and here he is— sitting on his bunk!"

It was too dark for me to see Wylie's face, but he tumbled rather than dismounted from his horse, and I felt him trembling as he brushed past me into the hut. I followed him, but during the single instant my back had been turned the rabbiter had moved. He was not on the bunk. Wylie kicked the logs into a blaze and then turned upon me fiercely. For the rabbiter was not in the hut at all.

"What d'ye mean," he roared, "by playing tricks on a chap who's lost his mate? Out of my hut, you young devil, out of my hut!" Never have I seen man more completely beside himself; he was shaking from head to foot in a perfect palsy, and his clenched fists were shaking in my face. I assured him I had played no conscious trick — it was my defective eyesight that must have played one on me. Now that I put on my glasses, I could see that the hut was empty but for our two selves; that it must have been absolutely empty till we entered. And yet, I could have sworn that I had seen the lost rabbiter nursing his face at the foot of that right-hand bunk.

My companion cooled down, however, on becoming convinced of my good faith, and instead of turning me out, seemed to set his heart upon explaining my 'fancied' vision before he would let me go. Pictures from the illustrated papers

106

had been tacked up over the rabbiter's bunk. One was the old coloured print of Red Riding Hood, with the four trees like an elephant's legs; and Wylie would have it that the firelight glowing on the child's hood had made the splotch of red which my nerves had exaggerated into a Crimean shirt.

To me this explanation seemed more ridiculous than the thing it sought to explain, but I had to admit that I could see but poorly without my glasses, and indeed I was very ready to confess to some inexplicable delusion on my part. So at that we left it, and I was glad enough to turn my back on the Five-mile hut, and to push on to the out-station at a hard-gallop.

Mr Armit, the owner, and Mr Mackeson, his manager, were still sitting up, discussing ways and means of coping with the long-continued drought; and the owner was good enough to praise my promptitude in coming to them at once. It was now midnight, and after a little consideration it was decided that we should all lie down for a bit, preparatory to starting back a couple of hours before daybreak in order to take part in the search. For my part, I made myself very comfortable before the fire, with my saddle as my pillow, and fell asleep in a moment. And in another, as it seemed to me, there was Mackeson laying hold of my shoulder and shouting in my ear that we were an hour late in starting as it was.

Our owner, however, had long been unaccustomed to the hardships of the bush, and when the time came he could not face the keen edge of the day without his pannikin of tea and his bite of 'browny'. So, the sun was on us before we were halfway back — not the red ball of nineteen out of twenty Riverina dawnings, but a copper disc like a new penny. Clouds of sand were whirling in the wind, which had risen greatly in the night, and was rising still; puffs of sand kept breaking from the plain to join the clouds; and we coughed, all three of us, as we cantered neck and neck.

"Do you think you could drive a whim, Forrester?" said Mr Armit, drawing rein as we sighted the Five-mile, and suddenly turning to me.

"I believe I could, Sir. I have seen one working, and it looks simple enough."

"It's as easy as it looks if you keep your tank nice and full and feed your troughs regularly. Wylie will show you all that is necessary in five minutes; the fact is, I think of leaving you in charge of this whim here since you can hardly know the paddocks well enough to be of much use in the search, whereas Wylie knows every inch of the run. What do you say, Mr Mackeson? It is for you to decide."

"I agree with you, Sir. But where's the whim got to?"

"Bless my soul!" gasped the other. "I was afraid we were in for a dust-storm, but I didn't think it would come so quick!"

Indeed, we were in the thick of the storm already. It was but a moment since hut and whim had disappeared in a whirl of deep yellow sand, and now we could see nothing at all beyond our horses' ears. Luckily, we were not many hundred yards from the hut.

"Give them their heads!" shrieked Mackeson, and, following his advice, we gained the hut before the sea of dust had choked us utterly. It literally tinkled on the corrugated roof, and we led in the horses after us, so terrible was the storm. The whim-driver lighted a slush lamp and put the billy on the fire to give us some tea. Everything in the hut wore a glistening yellow coat; there were layers of sand on our very eyelids, and what the owner squeezed from his beard alone made a little sandhill on the floor.

"Poor Powell!" he suddenly exclaimed. "This is the hardest luck of all upon him. It will blot out our tracks. It will double the agonies of thirst he must have already endured. I am very much afraid that it will destroy our last chance of finding him alive."

And Mr Armit looked reproachfully at the whim-driver, who was making the tea with his back turned to us, crouching over the fire in an attitude so humble and so disconsolate that it would have been inhuman as well as useless to find open fault with him now. For a few seconds there was silence in the hut, silence broken only by the continual tinkle on the roof, which, however, was louder than it had been. Then of a sudden the man at whom we were all looking wheeled round, sprang up, and pointed dramatically to the rattling roof.

"You are wrong— wrong— wrong!" cried he hoarsely. "Listen to that! That's not sand— that's rain! All the worst dust-storms end so; it'll rain the best part of an inch before it stops; instead of doing for him this'll — save — his— life!"

He looked from one to the other of us — half in triumph, half in terror still, I thought — then down on his knees and back to the boiling billy and the sugar and the tea. I saw him throw a handful of each among the bubbles — saw his fingers twitching as they spread—and I knew then that the whim driver's confidence was only lip-deep.

But a part of his prophecy came true enough. It rained until the crab-holes were full of water — until there was drink enough abroad upon the plains to give the whim a good week's holiday. Long before it stopped, however, I had the Five-mile hut to myself, with that dismal rattle on the roof, and a dull fire of damp logs spitting distressfully beneath the great square chimney. The troughs were not needed, and that was well, they were buried and hidden beneath a ridge of drifted sand, and I was to clear them with the long-handled shovel, instead of driving the whim.

I can still see those three horsemen bobbing into infinity behind the lances of the rain, and I see myself a lonesome, spindle-shanked figure, in leggings and breeches and the grey felt wideawake which still hangs on my wall; and I do not look very happy as I stand at the door of that hut, beneath the dripping corrugated eaves; but I do look a little elated and proud. I am going to spend days and nights in a hut five miles from any mortal soul, and I am young enough to appreciate playing Robinson Crusoe in earnest. It will be a good experience to put in the next letter home. A good experience!

The rain ceased before noon, when I had some lunch (for there was plenty to eat in Wylie's ration-bags), and then turned out with the long-handled shovel. My spirits rose in the open air. My own actions were less noisy and nerve-disturbing than I had found them in the lonely hut, and I could look all around me as I worked, without constantly foreseeing the hut door darkened by some apparition that might be welcome enough, but which must certainly startle me when it came. The events which I have already chronicled lay heavy on my nerves. I was only nineteen years of age, and I was cursed with an imagination.

Nothing, therefore, could have been better for me than the play I made during the next few hours with the long-handled shovel. Now and then I knocked off to rest my back and smoke a pipe; but once started, I stuck to my work pretty closely up to five o'clock by the old Waltham watch in the leather pouch on my belt. And it punished every muscle in my body; the shoulders felt it as I plunged the shovel into the heavy wet sand, the arms and shoulders as I swung it out loaded, while the strain upon back and legs was continuous. My task was the harder owing to the shovel having been bent and blunted by some misuse; yet, so far from loathing it, I was never prouder of anything than of the five-and-twenty yards of submerged trough which I uncovered and cleared that January afternoon.

To tire the body is the surest way of cleansing and purifying the mind, and I can honestly say that I returned to the hut without any morbid fancy in my head, indeed with no anxiety about anything but the fire, which I had foolishly forgotten. Judge, then, of the sensations with which I stood still on the threshold. The hut had no windows, but the afternoon had turned out very fine, the sun shone merrily through a hundred crevices, and there, on the foot of the same bunk, sat the lost rabbiter, precisely as I had seen him sitting the night before.

How long I stood, how long he remained, I do not know. I remember a hollow voice calling his name. I remember the pattering of my own tottering feet, my nerveless fingers clutching the empty air, my trembling body flung headlong on the other bunk, and the sobs that shook it as it lay. For then I knew that Henry Powell was already dead, and for the second time I had seen his ghost.

Not a particle of doubt remained in my mind. I could not be mistaken twice — I was perfectly certain that I had never been mistaken at all. This time, however, there was no dull red glow to play conceivable tricks in the darkness, for the fire was out, and it was almost as light in the hut as it was outside. Yet there I had seen him, in the self-same attitude, on the self-same spot, his hands covering his face, his beard showing between his wrists, his elbows planted on his thighs. I could have counted the checks in his Crimean shirt, and this time the glasses were still upon my nose.

Yes, I was absolutely certain of what I had seen, and that very certainly was now my consolation. The worst is worst of all before it happens; and the knowledge that I had seen a ghost was much more supportable than the doubt as to whether I had seen one or not. The ghost could not harm me, after all; instead of sympathising with myself I should grieve for the poor fellow who was already beyond the reach of succour.

111

Had they found him yet? Had they found the body? And, if so, would the whim driver return to his post at once and set me free? My heart beat fast with the hope, in defiance of my head. I might reason with myself that a poor ghost was no unfit companion, but how I longed to get away! Even then, however, my courage failed me in another place. Who would believe my yarn? So I stayed where I was— and have held my tongue till now.

Sundown roused me, for I must have my tea, ghost or no ghost, and to make tea I must relight the fire. Here an obstacle confronted and ultimately vanquished me. There was a wood-heap outside, but, of course, the wood was damp, and though I looked for the axe, to chop to the dry heart of the wet logs, I had not found it when night fell hastily, forcing me to abandon the search.

So I went without my tea, but ate with what appetite I had, and washed down the mutton and damper with pannikins of water from the nine-hundred-gallon tank outside. I had lighted the 'slush-lamp' (moleskin wick in tin of mutton fat), and I sat watching the foot of the dead man's bunk as I ate, but no further vision interrupted my meal. And afterwards, when I was smoking my pipe in the open air, I would look in every few minutes, and past where the light was burning, for I had an odd idea that I must see the apparition thrice. And I wish I had. Yet of what I saw twice I am as positive now as I was then.

It was a magnificent night: the rain had drawn the fever from the sun-baked plains, and left even that clear air clearer than I had known it yet. Every star was a diamond in the dark-blue vault, and my little pipe made the only clouds between earth and heaven. Often as I filled it, I had to light it still oftener at the flame which I had left burning in the hut, for I was rapt in thought. You are nowhere nearer to God than when alone in the bush beneath the undimmed tropic stars. I cannot

112

say what brought it home to me, or by what chain of thought I chanced on the conclusion, but all at once I stood still and knew that the hand of God was in the apparition which I had seen. It meant something. What did it mean? There must be some reason why I alone and not Wylie, for example, had been made to see the lost man sitting on his bunk. Then what could that reason be?

I thought, and thought, and thought, sauntering round and round the hut the while. At last, I entered, but not to light my pipe. I do not know what I meant to do; I only know what I did. I walked to the foot of Powell's bunk, and sat down where I had seen Powell sitting, with a vague feeling, I believe, that in that spot and in his own attitude my spirit might receive some subtle communication from that of the rabbiter. What I did receive was a tumble: for the foot of the bunk gave way beneath me. and I found myself deposited on the ground instead. Yet he, whom I had seen sitting there, had been in life a much heavier man than myself!

These bunks, or bush bedsteads, rather, are constructed upon universal and very simple lines. Four uprights are driven into the earth floor of the hut or tent, and then connected by horizontal poles with sack-cloth slung across. The result combines the merits of both bed and hammock; but the uprights must be firmly rooted in the ground, and I soon saw the explanation of the present downfall; the ground was all loose at the foot of the lost man's bed, and the outer upright had gone down like a ninepin beneath my weight.

For the moment I was merely puzzled. The ground had worn so hard elsewhere in the hut that I could not imagine why it should begin to crumble in this particular corner. I reached the slush-lamp and peered under the middle of the bed. There it was the same — as soft as a sandhill — but recently flattened with a shovel. I saw the concave marks. And suddenly I leant

113

back, and got up quickly, but with the perspiration running cold from every pore, for now I knew why the visible form of Henry Powell had appeared to me twice upon the foot of his bed. It was to tell me that his murdered remains lay buried beneath.

Now I knew why Wylie had pretended to be behindhand in bringing in his news: it was that we might think his mate really lost, and be ourselves so full of blame for an error of judgment that there should be no room in our minds for deadlier suspicions. Now I understood his rage and horror when I cried out that there was Powell come back —his subsequent anxiety to explain away my vision. And the missing axe— what had it done that he should hide it? And the long-handled shovel — I knew what had blunted and bent it now!

I remember mechanically looking at my watch, and yet not seeing the time. I remember looking again, and it was not quite half-past nine. The time goes so slowly when one is alone, and midnight begins so soon; but I was thankful it was earlier than I had thought. Now I could make sure — it would all be less ghastly than in the veritable dead of night — and then to the station with my news before anybody was in bed.

The miscreant Wylie! How well he had acted his diabolical part — in there at the men's hut — out here before the owner and the manager! Indignation at his bloody villainy became my first emotion, and it nerved me mightily. I tore away the poles and the sacking, and the soft earth rose in a mound — it had all been put back! I ran for the long-handled shovel, and, urged on by my boiling blood, I began to dig.

God knows how I went on! A boot stuck out first, and when I felt it there was a foot inside. It was scarce eighteen inches below the ground. Next I uncovered the Crimean shirt. That was enough for me. As I bent over it with the light, and blew away the sand, I saw here and there the red checks (no plainer than in my vision, however), but most of them were blotted out by a dark, stiff stain. I delved no deeper; this was indeed enough. I turned away, deadly sick, without rising from my knees, and there was Wylie himself watching me from the door!

I set the light down on the table — that, at any rate, was between us — and I looked up at him from my knees. He was glaring down on me with the most ferocious expression, every wrinkle writhing, and that loose pouch at his throat swelling as if with venom for spitting in my face. But, so far as I could see, he was unarmed; his bony right hand rested on what I took to be the handle of a stick, and, luckily, the long-handled shovel lay within reach of mine. I was the first to speak.

"I have found him," said I.

"More fool you."

"Why so? I am not frightened of you."

"Not frightened to die?"

"Not particularly; you'll follow me soon enough. One murder you could only conceal one day, and how long are you going to conceal two? Besides, you've got to kill me first."

And I was on my legs with the long shovel in both hands.

"That's soon done," he answered with a laugh, and then I saw my mistake. What I had taken for a mere stick was the missing axe; he must have hidden it somewhere outside and, after first catching me at work, stolen away and come back with it on tiptoe. Now he took two strides into the hut, and, as the axe came up over his shoulder and hung there, I saw bloodstains on the blade. The sight of them delayed me at the critical instant; yet I lunged as he struck, then started back, and the axe-head split through the table as though it had been a cigar-box. With a curse he wrenched it free, but I was on him first, and round and round we went, and over and over, until I had the wretch at my mercy in the very grave which has own hands had dug.

At my mercy because he lay as one paralysed when he found his body stretched out on that of his victim; but how long that would have lasted I do not care to conjecture. He was stronger than I, though less active, and I think that his strength must soon have come back tenfold. It had not done so when I caught the beat of the sweetest music I have ever heard — the music cf eight cantering hoofs drawing nearer and nearer to the hut.

The slush-lamp had fallen and gone out when the axe fell, but my eyes were searching for that villain's eyes in the darkness, and I would have given something to see them as the music fell on his ears too — as the horsemen's spurs jingled on the ground outside and then in the hut.

"Is Wylie here, Forrester?" cried the manager's voice.

"He is."

"We suspect him of having murdered Powell himself!"

"He has done so. Strike a light and you shall see them both."

But at the trial I said nothing of my two visions, for, as I have stated, I had not then the moral courage, and the case was complete without that. My story began when the bed collapsed beneath me — that was all —so terrified was 1 of making myself a discredited laughing-stock. Now I do not care, nor do I think there will be so many disbelievers. At all events I have relieved my mind by telling the whole truth at last — so help me God.

This I think irrelevant, but those who are interested, and who do not know it, may be glad to learn that Wylie the whim-driver lived to die as he deserved.

The Burrawurra Brand

The Burrawurra run had many merits, but those of the homestead in the midst of it were few and adventitious. The site was central, certainly, for you might strike the boundary by riding out ten miles in any direction; and it was conspicuous, because, no matter what direction you chose, you had to cover at least three miles of open plain before finding shelter from the Riverina sun. Nor was there any shade at the homestead itself, save the clean-cut shadows of the various buildings. A crooked pine-tree wasted in the station-yard, but only one; itself, and the white-washed walls and beams and verandah posts surrounding it, were all that remained of the original clump. Above the whitewashed walls was an acre or two of galvanised iron in small allotments. So from a distance, the homestead greatly resembled a group of packing cases with tin lids, and in itself it did not attract. But old George Wade, who both owned and managed Burrawurra, made you glow before you got there, from the warmth of remembered welcomes and the certainty of a warm one in store; and Mrs Wade was wonderfully glad to see you, for an invalid lady who had no business in the bush; and young George was a genial villain, but it was his sister that you went to see. For a white frock fluttering in the verandah at Burrawurra homestead was as a lighthouse light flashing over the sea. Good eyes could discern it across miles of sand and salt-bush, and those that did so without delight were looking for the first time upon Pinkie Wade.

Not that Pinkie was a beauty; she was less than that, and also more. She was wiry and thin and rather tall, with the hand and stride of a man, and a smile more audacious than winning, though one was glad enough to have it just as it was. And her smile was all her own. It began in her eyes, cleverness was needed to know when, for these were so dark that there was no defining the pupils, which made their expression often inscrutable; and it ended in a gleaming show of teeth, just as it became very hard to stand away from her lips any longer. But the best has been said. Her colour was distinctly sallow. Her face was leaner than is looked for in a girl. She disfigured her forehead with a coal-black fringe, and her speech with a twang that nobody could admire. Sometimes she disfigured it much more dreadfully: once, at all events, she had been heard to use certain crisp expressions to some killing-sheep she had undertaken to pen, which being reported to her mother, Pinkie shed tears of penitence, but pleaded provocation. The tears were a rarity, and let us hope the cause was, too. Pinkie, however, showed tenderness at all times to her poor mother: but she had no tenderness for her admirers, of which she might have thought herself lucky to own one in the bush, instead of the four or five who would ride from ten to forty miles for the pleasure of being snubbed by her.

Yet she liked them much, and she liked them all, and when they came to her one at a time, she very nearly loved each in turn, for each was good of his kind. There was Shaw, the Government Surveyor, who was very honest and pleasant and good-humoured, besides being as thoroughly colonial as Pinkie herself. There was young Hutton, the new chum at Yellow Plains, who was amusing because he was so very much in earnest. There was a Rabbit Inspector, with a good English name and a beautiful moustache, and a fallen angel's air of melancholy badness which Pinkie found more irresistible every time he came, and he was beginning to come very often. Then there was John Hartley, of Gunbar, and Gunbar is a finer station than Burrawurra, besides being John Hartley's own.

He, too, was delightful, as a devotee twice her age generally is to a girl of twenty. The younger the man the less his chance, so in this case young Hutton had the least chance of them all, in spite of his pathetic mentionings of the money he had for investment, and of his preference for a station life beyond all others. Even young Hutton, however, was good to see when none of the others came, for he was proud in his boyish way, and he had more imagination than the rest of them put together, and would talk better when alone with her. Any one of the four, in fact, was delightful by himself. But at last a malignant fate brought all four to Burrawurra on the same Saturday, and the result was extraordinary.

It was the beginning of December and hot enough to grill chops in ten minutes on the verandah roof. This is on the authority of Pinkie Wade, who said it to her mother while placing an eau-de-Cologne pad on the poor lady's forehead, and fanning her afresh. Mrs Wade always did fall ill at the commencement of the very hot weather, and she had fallen ill now while her husband was away buying horses. Pinkie was looking after her, and it was from her mother's window that she beheld John Hutton's buggy drive up, to her dismay. The interesting Inspector followed at three in the afternoon, and Shaw, the Surveyor, before five, when, as it grew cooler, Mrs Wade actually came out to see her guests. She would not have them know how ill she was, nor did they guess. Such is the hospitality of the squatter and his wife.

But Pinkie was extremely angry, and when young Hutton arrived, after a ride of five-and-twenty miles, in time for supper, she happened to be the first person he saw, and her anger broke loose. She told him what was the matter, and asked him, ridiculously, why on earth he had chosen this day of all days. His answer was to wheel round his horse as if to remount, whereupon Pinkie Wade seized the reins with one

119

hand and snatched the spectacles from his nose with the other. He was a near-sighted new chum.

"What are you up?" she cried, really angrily now.

"Let me go back," he answered doggedly, giving her a curious stare without his glasses, and holding out his hand for them. But Pinkie Wade fixed them on her own nose, and pretended that she could see him through them, with her head on one side.

"I'll let you *walk* back if you lose your temper!" she said, most unjustifiably. "You're to stay and amuse the others. I shan't see anything of you, so I hope you'll keep out of mischief and not quarrel. You shall play tennis all day long tomorrow; you're to stay just to make up a four — otherwise you shouldn't. Here, take back the things, I can't see through 'em."

And the smile ended as it always did, Hutton whipping on his glasses to see the last of it, and each dazzling tooth was as a new nail in the coffin of his peace of mind. But he might have rested in thankfulness and good hope. For not so familiarly would she have treated any of the others, and whatever familiarity may breed, it is itself bred by the kind of feelings that would have encouraged young Hutton had he divined them in Pinkie Wade.

It was in his favour, however, that there were four of them to play lawn-tennis next day, without young Wade, who had things to see to; for in spite of his eyesight, Hutton was the best of the four; and in spite of Mrs Wade's indisposition, which continued, Pinkie came out to watch the games. The play was not of a high order, certainly, but neither was she to know that. She did not pretend to know much about it. She merely saw the new chum from Yellow Plains repeatedly put the ball past the handsome Rabbit Inspector, who had gone to the devil before lawn-tennis was invented, and picked up his play in the

120

infernal regions that had harboured him now for some years. His play was bad, and his temper turned out to be rather bad also; and when Pinkie discovered this, the fascination of a vaguer and more attractive kind of badness became cancelled for the time. She followed Hutton's good strokes with the most provoking applause, which had the double effect of improving his play and demoralising that of the Inspector. But the Inspector was by no means a bad fellow in one sense of the term. The other Englishman's better play, and Pinkie Wade's vexatious plaudits, combined to irritate him at the moment, but he was perfectly good-natured in the evening. Good-natured also was the chaff that then went on, whereof fragments floated to Pinkie's ears. But she chose to think otherwise, because she could hear just enough to know that the new chum was the person who was being chaffed. The new chum always is that person. In most cases he merits all the chaff he gets. In most cases, also, he stands it charmingly, though chaff in the bush is a rusty rapier with a jagged blade. Hutton stood his as he was likely to stand it, coming as he did (and not so long since) from a public school. But Pinkie heard what she did hear with an absurd sense of indignation. She was just feminine enough to be hopelessly unfair in her judgment of others, and from that night her fallen angel was also her fallen idol. Nor was he ever picked up or put together again, though somebody did his best, for there are some things that women would never believe, though the Recording Angel signed an affidavit to their truth.

Nevertheless, the visitation of the four would at least have ended peacefully, and been given a decent burial in the mind of Pinkie Wade, but for a circumstance of pure chance, the like of which would not happen twice. On a station only one horse is stabled overnight — the night-horse — which is used for running up the others from the horse-paddock at break of day. When the four said goodnight to Pinkie Wade, three of them

121

made it goodbye, fully intending to be away before breakfast next morning; and the fourth, John Hartley, who was himself in no hurry, followed their example after a moment's hesitation, and in obedience to a sportsman-like instinct which did him credit. But two horses were somehow missed by the man who ran up the rest; it turned out later that a fence was broken, and they had got adrift in another and a larger paddock; but the odd thing was that the missing two were the nags of young Hutton and the Inspector of rabbit-skins. The sun grew fierce, and these horses had not been found. Young George Wade persuaded the two to stay, in any case, till the cool of the evening. John Hartley, who had never wanted to make an early start, elected to wait also, and Shaw, the Surveyor, who also was his own boss, naturally followed suit. Genial young Wade, who had work to do in a distant corner of Burrawurra run, postponed that also until the blessed evening. So five healthy men were left with the thermometer already rising 110° in the shade and a long morning on their idle hands. And Satan was their man.

From whom the suggestion came, there is no saying at this distance of time. They were squatting in the store verandah, vagariously yarning, and it probably arose from talk concerning the late shearing. The suggestion was that they should all turn into the store and cut each other's hair, and it was carried by acclamation.

Now the store was a building by itself, and knew neither partitions nor sub-divisions of any kind. It was a large, low, dingy-looking place, but roomy enough, in spite of its multifarious contents. These included all reasonable wants of the wilderness, stowed away on shelves, depending from the beams, or preserved in cases and barrels. Hutton noticed the stencil of the Burrawurra brand hanging from a nail, the Burrawurra brand being W over 60 — W for Wade, and 60 for

122

the sixty thousand sheep the station would carry in good seasons. He noticed it professionally, because he personally had wielded such another brand during the recent shearing at Yellow Plains. Later, the Burrawurra brand became horribly familiar to him. For it was painted in white on two casks that stood side by side in one corner of the store. One of these casks contained lime-juice, the other whisky. A single glass was found, and as each man rose with a cropped head from the victim's chair, the whole party adjourned, with the glass, to that corner, where whisky and lime-juice was swiftly swallowed, with no allaying rain. This refreshment between the acts was really the inspiration of a naturally thirsty soul, the Inspector, but the new chum thought it was a custom of the bush. They told him that, and he believed it; there are stranger customs, if you come to think of it. Now the new chum disliked lime-juice, and he was only beginning not to dislike whisky. Nor did he love the expedition with which he was made to toss off the fluid (because of the one glass only), although, indeed, he had no desire to let it trickle over his palate in a succession of drops. But he did love, more than most things, a custom of the bush; the phrase alone charmed him; and he drank more than once to the honour of the public schools, coupled with the names of Eton and Rugby, the Rabbit Inspector's school and his own.

So it came to pass that when Pinkie came into the store about half-past eleven, to say a word to her brother, she saw the hair of Hutton's head (which had not yet been cut) peeping over some sacks of flour. An instinct had made young Hutton hide. Another instinct, when the girl was gone — as he fancied, without seeing that she was still there — made him desire to break away from the hair-cutting altogether. He said that he was going to see whether his horse had been run up yet, and if so he was off to Yellow Plain, as after all he had better

123

get back there as soon as possible. The proposal was resisted, but young Hutton stood to his guns. It was a last stand; his horse was not yet in the yard. He returned to the store, for where else could he go? Pinkie's frock fluttered in the verandah of the main building, but yet another instinct told him that she would not receive him kindly at that moment. He concentrated his mind on walking back to the store as an arrow flies, and flattered himself that he entirely succeeded.

The third victim was shaking the hair from his winding sheet as young Hutton entered. He was in time for his ration of whisky and lime-juice, which he stoutly refused. He said that the lime-juice was getting into his boots. Whereupon pressure was brought to bear on him in the name of the public schools which appealed to his pride. Once more the unholy blend made Hutton wince, as he tossed it off in the dark corner where the great twin barrels stood. That corner was so dark that each man mixed his own by guess-work, but the Burrawurra brand grinned from each barrel in the white paint that defied the darkness; and the grin broadened as Hutton put down his empty glass.

The order of the hair-cutting was *seniores priores*, as Hutton remarked with an unction which was accepted as a proof that he had really been at Rugby. Young Wade, from the chair, entreated a translation, which the new chum gave him with an adjectival freedom which was a proof, on the other hand, that he had also been some time in the bush. His turn came next (he was denied his turn as operator), and, as he began to feel, the sooner the better. But before it came, his spectacles fell from his nose, and he himself stamped upon them with ferocious mirth until the lenses were ground to powder. That obviously was the lime-juice that was in his boots. At his next interview with the Burrawurra brand he was panting with excitement, but without his glasses he could not see what he was doing, and the taps were stiff to turn. He is afraid he must have abused the Burrawurra brand, and the man who cut his hair is careful to make a point of it that he did.

He knows that he fell asleep while his hair was being cut. The last thing he remembers hearing distinctly was the voice of John Hartley (who was preparing to go, and who was old enough not to have been there at all) saying that something was a shame. Also he felt something cold upon his neck, besides the scissors. But he slept until they made him get up, having finished with him. They then asked him (as it seemed to him, through telephones) how he felt as to the back of his head; and he replied as to his feelings generally, with a candour that was admirable, though needless.

"Rugby," said he Rabbit Inspector, "you want another drink!"

"Eton," began Hutton —   And his language to the Etonian was thick in more senses than one.

Remember that this orgy was a morning performance. That is its sole claim to distinction. It was half-past twelve, with a shade temperature of 112° Fahrenheit, when the performers vacated the store in a body, leaving (like the sheep of Little Bo-peep, herself a squatter's daughter) their hair behind them. Nothing further occurred, save instances of how badly and well men may treat a man during one and the same hour. But the story went forward at luncheon, and on his account.

Pinkie Wade asked where he was, and fixed her black eyes upon the handsome Rabbit Inspector. Now the Inspector had a head on him like a lump of quartz, but this did not prevent him being in the best of humours, thanks to everything, and he answered airily that the new chum had been in the sun, which had proved too much for him. As the girl continued to stare at him very hard, he added that the thermometer stood at some hundreds in the shade.

125

Then the Rabbit Inspector, who had been educated at Eton, received from Miss Wade of Burrawurra a reprimand which he cannot have forgotten to this day, though he was the man to forgive it. She divined what had really happened, and spoke out with a moral fearlessness which the Inspector himself could not help admiring. John Hartley had gone and she blamed the Inspector only, with a fine injustice which had yet enough justice in it to make her charges impossible to answer. Her worst charge she kept to herself; it was so monstrously unfair that, had she uttered it, out of her own mouth would she have armed the Inspector for his self-defence. As it was he merely returned her stare — and his own was not free from dignity — while young Wade sat in stupid silence, and the Government Surveyor hung his head. The girl's words cut their dulled ears like knives, but the ears of the Inspector were not so dull, belonging, as they did, to a head of quartz. When she paused he bowed slightly; then he rose from his chair so abruptly that he knocked it over, but Pinkie Wade was nimbler, and she was out of the room before him.

"Old man," gasped the girl's brother, finding his voice at last, "I'm — I'm damnably ashamed of her!"

"My good fellow," replied the Inspector, who had at least gone to the devil a gentleman, "you ought to be proud of her. She was a bit rough, but between us we deserved every word, and, by God, she can hit out straight!"

But he rode away, and Shaw followed him in his buggy, steering an unsteady course that Pinkie watched with a curled lip from her mother's bedside, where she sat plying a fan with so gentle a hand that Mrs Wade slept beneath the soft current of cool air.

Young Wade saw his friends off with a long face, and further apologies, which the Inspector again tossed back in his face. "She's a stunner," he said, as he rode away. But George

126

could not see his sister in that light just then. He would have to face her later. It occurred to him to turn out Hutton's horse, which had been run up at last, so that at least he would have one man to stand by him that night. But before night, he had to perform the duty neglected in the morning; that duty called him to a distant quarter of the run; and before he could obey this call he felt it necessary, for many reasons, to lie down and sleep. So he went to his room, which Hutton was sharing with him because of the visitation of the four together, and lay down there.

When Hutton awoke, which was barely before sundown, he discovered somebody sitting on the edge of the other bed and putting on his spurs. He guessed that it was George Wade, but he could see nothing distinctly without his glasses; and when he felt for them he began to remember things. He lay still for some moments. The universe was inside his head, George Wade stood up, and his spurs tinkled on the floor.

"Where are you going?" said Hutton.

"Hallo!" cried George. "How are you?"

"As fit as I deserve to be. It's not saying much. Where are you off to?"

George's answer brought Hutton into a bolt upright position on the bed. "Surely you aren't going to leave a fellow?" he said nervously. "Wait for me, and we'll start together."

"My dear boy, you're not going tonight," said young Wade, comfortably; "don't you believe it."

"I must!" cried Hutton, springing to his feet.

"Why must you? Anyway, you can't, because your horse isn't in yet," affirmed George Wade, unblushingly; "he's got through into a big paddock, and it'll take me a time to find him. I'll have a look for him this evening; I shan't be out so long."

"Shall you be back to supper?" asked Hutton wistfully.

"Well, no; I'm going to get a snack with a boundary rider, who was expecting me this morning. I must go and see him tonight."

"Then I must go, too. Lend me a horse, George, for God's sake!"

"Why, man?"

"Because — I can't face — your sister. She'll know all about it!"

"She knows nothing," vowed the immoral George. "Even if she did, do you suppose it would matter?"

"Well, I shouldn't like to look her in the face again," said Hutton, and the touch of pride in his tone passed the other's comprehension. George, indeed, burst out laughing.

"My good chap, it's nothing new to her!" he cried, little knowing how it horrified Hutton to hear this. "She's seen it before. She's used to it. She wouldn't think any the worse of you. After all, you were only the worst of a bad lot; and she'll think you were the best, because she saw us others. Honour bright, she did! So cheer up and don't be off your smoke when I get back; I promise you I won't be late."

Hutton looked into young Wade's eyes to see whether he was telling the truth, but his own were half blind for the want of glasses, and it was more natural to him at his age to believe than to disbelieve. He believed and gave in.

Hutton walked over to the stockyard with Wade, and saw the last of him, as George had seen the last of the others, but with an even longer face. George's last words were an inquiry after the back of Hutton's head. Hutton said it felt as though it had been very badly cropped, and George was laughing as he rode away in the gloaming. This young man had certainly no morals.

Poor Hutton went back to his room and dipped his head in cold water a great many times; between the times he made as elaborate a toilet as the contents of his valise would permit. The loss of his glasses was another handicap. But when he emerged into the open air he was looking very sleek; his hair in front seemed nicely cut, though it was rather too wet; his coat was scrupulously brushed. No sooner, however, was he in the station yard, than his heart began knocking, for in the verandah outside the dining-room door he could see something white, and even without his spectacles he knew that it was Pinkie Wade. He stepped boldly forward, taking heart of what George had told him. But the moment he set foot in the verandah where she was, he knew that George had lied to him. He knew it from the way in which she rose from her chair as he drew near. He knew it from the tone of her voice, though she only said "Good evening" to him.

Her leant against a verandah post, and tried to say more to her, and not to think of George. But it was very hard to find anything to say, and perhaps she purposely made it harder. Also, he had his thoughts, and his mind was steeped in remorse. Pinkie was in one of her snow-white frocks, whose purity made his own evil performance the more black and awful in his eyes. You see, he had imagination. It was one of the things she liked in him. But it was a thing that added much to his misery at this moment, for his thoughts flew to his own womenkind in England, while his eyes rested upon Pinkie Wade, and he was young enough to wonder what they would have thought.... But supper put an end to these speculations; only to give him a new lease of discomfiture on still more embarrassing terms.

For he and Pinkie had to face one another across the length of the cloth, so that he could hardly see her at all, and no other face was at the table. He had to carve for her, and this he managed to do in spite of his blindness; but having carved for himself also, he found himself quite unable to eat. His inability

129

was conspicuous. Pinkie expressed a fear that the mutton was underdone, and proposed the cold joint. He said he did not think he could eat anything. He was foolish enough to add that he didn't know why, for Pinkie said promptly —

"I do!"

"I hope you don't." he cried, losing his head.

"Why, surely, there is no disgrace in being overcome by the sun? That, they tell me, happened to you this morning. I was very sorry to hear it," Pinkie Wade said, sadly.

"You were sorry?" asked Hutton, wildly.

"I was grieved," she whispered.

He sprang to his feet, and history repeated itself, for he knocked over his chair in his nervous haste. He blundered to the door, and there turned round.

"You know what happened!" he blurted out. "I can't see your face, but I can tell that you know, from your voice. I am more ashamed of myself than I have ever been in my life before. But I won't ask you to forgive me, because I don't deserve to be forgiven!"

He looked towards her for a moment with shame and penitence, and the wistful yearning that comes into eyes that would but cannot see distinctly. In his, the girl thought that there were tears as well. But she liked him for being too proud to ask her forgiveness, and he was gone before she could be sure of the tears. Ere she had time to follow him to the door a mist had come before her own eyes, and for some moments she, too, could not see. She listened behind the door, and heard him go into his room at the other side of the station-yard. When he came out she wiped her eyes, and watched through the crack of the open door. He had his valise under his arm, and he disappeared in the direction of the stock-yard. Then Pinkie Wade began to wring her hands and to vilify the poor Inspector whom lately she had inclined to worship.

"It was all your doing," she muttered viciously, "you brute! But I'll never look at you again — never! You thought I'd never look at *him* again, did you? Pooh, I have always liked him twice as well as you, though you are so fine and large, and now I know it. He's got to be forgiven, but *you*...."

The Rabbit Inspector troubled her thoughts no more just then; but her mind was made up about him for good and all. It was one of those cases in which a woman condemns a man on strong circumstantial evidence; she always hangs him. Pinkie stepped forth into the station-yard, and smiled at the moon, which was rising over the roof that had just covered her. I don't say it was the case, but possibly her smile had to do with her own appearance in the white moonlight and that white dress. Conceivably, too, the frown that followed her smile was caused by the recollection that the new chum from Yellow Plains had either lost or broken his glasses. But these are deep waters. It is certain, on the other hand, that light steps now crossed the sandy tract dividing the cluster of tin-lidded buildings from the stock-yard; that they hesitated halfway, when a figure became visible leaning dejectedly through the stock-yard rails, with its back to the homestead; and that a few moments later this figure started and shivered as if an arrow had lodged between its shoulder-blades, instead of the finger of a girl.

"What are you doing here?" the girl said.

"I am waiting for my horse," replied the figure.

"Why, your horse won't be run up till morning!"

"I am waiting here till morning."

"But why?" she asked him, with genuine concern; and then he turned upon her with his hungry eyes, and she recoiled from him.

"Because I have made a disgrace and a fool of myself," he cried bitterly; "because I have made a beast of myself in your

131

house and abused your hospitality, so that I will never set foot here again! This is the brutal English of it; I'll ask your pardon for the English, if you like; but never for what is unpardonable. Here I stick till I get my horse. Then I am off, and you will never see me any more!"

To her his pride seemed splendid; it did not occur to her that a proper pride would have been proud before the event. She was a little unsophisticated with all her arts.

"I think it was very unkind of you to say that," she said, dolefully, "I — we all — like you very much."

"Then you will have the goodness to hate me this instant," cried Hutton, vigorously. "If you knew how I hate myself!" he added in his misery.

"That's absurd.... After all — perhaps we're savages — but it isn't such a very out-of-the-way thing up in these parts.... And then, you know, it wasn't your fault!"

Until she said this, he was softening. He was closer to her than he realised, because his only desire was to see her plainly once more, and his sight was very short without his glasses. He was feasting his eyes on her until she told him it was not his fault. At that he flung himself upright with a gesture of indignation.

"Don't say that," he said sharply. "It *was* my fault. Nobody else was in the least to blame. Such things are only one man's fault, or else he is not a man at all!"

She did not agree with him. But she did like his pride more and more until she was beginning to love it, and to lose her own. For now her hand lay lightly on his arm — it was a firm arm, though lean — and she was telling him, in a voice that trembled, not to be an old stupid, but to come back to the house instead of offending them all.

"I care nothing about the others," he said brusquely. "I have offended myself — and you!"

132

"You care nothing about me," she whispered, with her eyes once more close to his, and burning into them. "You care only about yourself. I am nobody."

"You are everybody."

"How can I believe you?"

His eyes melted into hers, and at last his arms showed her how she might believe him.... And that is the end of this discreditable episode, save that one of Pinkie's hands, not knowing what to do with itself, caressed the back of his head. Whereupon she broke away from him crying —

"Turn round, and let me look at you."

He turned round.

"Take off your hat and throw back your head."

He did both. She had made him turn his back to the moon as well as to her. Suddenly he saw her shadow bobbing up and down on the sand in front of him. She was laughing alarmingly.

"What on earth's the matter with you?" cried Hutton, facing about; and it is lamentable to note the difference in his tone to her at this early stage of their engagement, which was just three minutes old.

"Who cut your hair?" demanded Pinkie Wade.

"That's mentioning what we were never to mention again, and — and I really couldn't tell you."

"You poor boy! It doesn't much matter who he was, or whether he used the stencil or not. But the Burrawura brand is W over 60, and he's cut it in your back-hair as plain as ever I saw it on a bale o' wool!"

The man that shot Macturk

The morning after my arrival at Gong-gong, in the colony of Victoria, an odd thing happened as I was dressing. My bedroom opened on one end of the verandah, which a man was sweeping when I rose. No other soul was in sight from the window; so I flung wide the door, meaning to air myself for a moment in my pyjamas, for the night had been hot; and as a matter of course I said "Good morning" to the man. He stared at me for perhaps three seconds. Then his broom clattered in the verandah, and he had taken to his heels without a word or a cry.

"Well!" I said at last. I had been trying, unsuccessfully (for I had barely glanced at the fellow), to recall his features: now I went to the glass and examined my own. I looked no worse than what I was — a man warm from his bed. The red rust was out upon my cheeks and chin; it is there every morning of my life; and I could swear that my appearance was no more repulsive than that of the average man whose entire toilet is in front of him. I shrugged hopelessly as I shut the door. There was no trace of my man, save his broom lying where he had let it drop. It was still there when I came forth clothed and clean, half an hour later, and proceeded to the breakfast-room, armed to the teeth with my topic.

Mrs Spurling was pouring out the tea when I spoke of it. She looked so hard at me that the cup she was filling overflowed. Her husband stared, too, and I began to feel thankful that the three of us were alone. For now I made certain that something had gone radically wrong with me in the night — something that a man would be the last to discern in himself. In the height of my embarrassment the lady said to her husband:

"Did you notice it last night, John?"

"Never till this moment, my dear."

"Yet the likeness is the strongest — "

Here I broke in with a laugh of pure relief.

"For pity's sake, Mrs Spurling," I cried, "tell me whom it is that I am like, for I was beginning to fancy it must be the — well, let us say the fiend himself."

"A fiend you are certainly like," said Mrs Spurling, smiling. "But I am bound to say, he was the best-mannered and nicest-looking fiend I ever heard of," she added, in a manner that might have renewed my embarrassment, had it not caught my interest on the rebound.

I looked from the lady to her husband and back again at the wife with an intentionally wry face. They were an elderly couple, who had had no children, but a number of adventures instead, in the earlier days of the Colony. This had made their conversation unusually interesting overnight. Was I starting the morning within reach of a further adventure, worth all the rest put together? At any rate, my own apparent likeness to some more or less diabolical person unknown was in itself a highly exhilarating circumstance, and one on which a little curiosity seemed justifiable on my part. Presently I said as much, in as many words; and Mrs Spurling answered me, after a moment's hesitation.

"The fact is," she said, "you are startlingly like a notorious gentleman who once, many years ago, spent a night with us in this very room."

"A bushranger?" I asked quickly.

"A bushranger and a murderer. He made me play to him on that piano. And be slept on that sofa— with one eye open!"

My eyes, however, were not yet for the sofa or the piano, but for John Spurling, squatter, whose own were on his plate. He was a steady-going, slightly sombre man, with a brilliant diamond ring that looked strangely out of keeping on his gnarled finger; and now for the first time I noticed him touch and look at it, as if suddenly reminded it was there. He had also struck me as silent, save when wound up for yarning, for which he had a turn. But he had solemnly assured me that he could boast of no personal experiences of bushrangers, and he evidently remembered having said so, for he looked up at me at last with a little laugh.

"My wife has given me away; but the fact is, we have almost made it a rule, for reasons of our own, not to talk — "

Here I interposed with a sincere apology. But now they would not listen to me.

"Not at all, not at all," said the squatter, with a smile. "We have saddled you with a most unflattering likeness, and you are entitled to know something about your double."

"And why poor Pat turned tail at the sight of you," added Mrs Spurling, as she handed me the sugar and the milk.

"Ah! we must hunt him up after breakfast," said her husband. "And after breakfast I'll spin you the yarn; only — not that we mind, but for poor Pat's sake — you mustn't repeat it in this district, for it's just beginning to be forgotten about here."

I gave the necessary promise; but this is not that district.

Gong-gong Station is somewhere or other among the northern spurs of the Plenty Ranges. My stay there was but for two nights, many years ago now, and I have never been able to discover the spot on any map. On the other hand, I can still see the morning view from the front verandah, whence one's eyes

136

went helter-skelter down a grassy slope till they were stopped by posts and rails; whereupon they took a forest at one bound, and landed on the highest peak of the smoke-blue range opposite. I see the clouds our pipes put into the cloudless sky, and Mrs Spurling knitting on one side of me while her husband held forth on the other. At this moment his voice rings in my memory — so sharply that I feel as though I had taken up my pen to write at his dictation— and with the yarn comes the click of my lady's needles in accompaniment. Nor have I since laid eyes on two better comrades than this sere and yellow couple, whose stoutest bond was the memory of the hardships and the adventures through which they had seen one another in the rough old days.

Mr Spurling began with a little hit at me, after certain questions on his side and certain admissions on mine.

"Here's a man who is inquisitive about bushrangers," said he, looking at his wife and pointing at me; "yet he means to tell me he never heard of Burke, or Ben Hall, or Captain Melville— let alone Macturk! My boy you've never heard of the pick of the whole bushranging basket! The Kellys were no fools at it, I grant you, but they came later, and they came by themselves. Thunderbolt, too, was a bit behind the times, and neither he nor Captain Moonlight could compare with the boys of the fifties and sixties. Those were the palmy days of bushranging, the days of the men I've mentioned— and you never heard of. Burke and Macturk were done for in succeeding years; and I saw the last of poor Macturk. Burke was a brute: he robbed the New South Wales mail three times in twelve weeks, which was fine enough in the way of business; but the Diamond Creek murder, which hanged him in the end, was not. I'll tell you about that afterwards. It was a cold-blooded, beastly crime; Macturk couldn't have committed it, and Ben Hall wouldn't. He never touched your money

137

unless you had plenty, didn't Ben Hall. And all that lot, including Burke himself, were the devil's own gentlemen where ladies were concerned — took off their hats and played the gallant highwayman of the olden time. But for all that sort of thing— for dash that wasn't all bullying bounce, and devilry with a divine moment hers and there— Macturk was the boy, and none other within a cooee of him! He was a gentleman! But he had also been a murderer — though strictly in the way of business, mind — not like Burke— and there was a price upon his head. Dead or alive, he was worth a couple of hundred pounds to the man that nabbed him. And with those two hundred on his head, and placarded in every township throughout the colony, he turns up here one fine evening, to spend the night, just as you did yesterday!"

"Didn't you know who he was?" I asked.

"He made no secret of that."

"Pray go on!"

"He turned up about sundown, as my wife and I were sitting where we are now; and he hung up his horse to that post, and cooked up one foot on the edge of the verandah here (he wore jack-boots and thundering long spurs that set me thinking), and told us who he was as cool as rain, and that what he wanted most was a night's entertainment and a fresh horse to go on with next day. Now listen to me. The fellow's name was a byword in the country. His character was as well-known as any other public man's and a vast deal more popular! I am ashamed to say that he was absurdly idolised after death by a considerable section of the community; yet I'm bound to add that my wife and I, for one — which is not the bull it sounds, young man — were not altogether surprised at the fact. You'll hear our why and wherefore in a moment; meanwhile, I was telling you about his character. Report had it he was as mild as milk where there was no resistance, and as sweet as honey into the bargain where a lady was concerned; but where fight was shown, not fifty petticoats would have stopped the bloodshed. That was the beggar's reputation. Then imagine yourself a married man, and tell me what you would have done in my place?"

I made the only answer. "Nothing, I suppose. What did you do?"

The reply came from Mrs Spurling; along with a rosy glow which made me see her as a girl, and a fine one too.

"He just took me on his knee," said she, "and asked the bushranger to step-up and sit down in the empty chair!"

"Which he did," said Mr. Spurling hastily. "And here sat the three of us, and started chatting like the best friends in the world."

"'I don't see any men about, saving your presence,' says he, looking right and left, very sudden. 'What's got the crew?'

"'My men's hut is a quarter of a mile off— the way you didn't come,' I told him; 'besides, they've been mustering, and aren't all in yet.'"

"'And when'll they all be in, think you?' says he.

"'Oh, give 'em till half-past seven.'

"'Sure?' he cries, like cocking a revolver.

"'Quite,' says I. 'Can't you see that I'm a married man?'

"'I can,' he says, 'and not a hair of your beard shall be touched, old man, if you'll do me reasonably for this one night and mount me decently in the morning. No spavins, mind!' says he. Then he pulls out his watch, and says, 'It isn't seven, yet,' and asks Mrs Spurling if he may smoke a cigar, and offers me one first, as polite as a new-chum governor. A cigar in the bush! You bet it was a prime one, too; and as for his watch, it was a gold repeater, and where it and the cigar came from I felt mighty inquisitive to know, but didn't just like to ask. There were so many things you wanted to ask him about! Such a

139

chap he was from head to toe! Confound his impudence! How I wish that I could make you see the fellow as we see him in our minds, don't you, my dear?" This to his wife.

"It must be so difficult for you to realise," said Mrs Spurling, looking up at me without holding her busy hands. "I could never believe there had been such a man, if we hadn't had him here. There was never another quite like him. That we do know. Yet you remind me of him in everything but your expression."

"And his dress!" chimed in Mr Spurling. "He wore a diamond ring," proceeded the squatter (whose own was at the moment thrust inside his coat with his right hand), "and had no end of finery concealed about his person. His cigar case was solid silver, and he had two Albert chains to his repeater. But he wasn't a fool, like Thunderbolt, or one of them, who had pierced ears, and would always wear the earrings he had stolen— a fresh pair for each day of the week. Macturk had taste. His breeches fitted him like a glove, his linen was cleaner than mine, and he'd picked up a cabbage- tree hat that would have gone into your waistcoat-pocket— never saw such a cabbage- tree before or since! Then he must have carried a razor in his swag, for his chin was as smooth as yours. His shirt was the least bit open at the neck, whether for coolness or vanity I can't say, but it was the best bit of connection between a fine head and splendid shoulders that ever I saw in my life. He had an Adam's apple like a billiard-ball, I recollect— don't you, my dear ?— and ears like a woman's. And you could have stuck a shilling in the cleft of his chin, and – and – "

"Oh, John!" said Mrs Spurling. "But it was a very strong face, and not a bad one, by any means. We were the whole night studying it, you must remember."

"We were so! I was coming to that. Halfway through his cigar, he asks to see the store. Now, we've no use for a great

140

big store on a little place like this, and you might stay here for a week without guessing where our store is. It's in the very centre of the house, with no outer wall, but a bit of a skylight instead of windows, and only one door, which opens off the room where we've just had breakfast. Mind, the place is a store in the pure and simple sense of the word— it isn't an office, like most station stores. I don't have my desk in there, or the station books, or anything of that sort. But I *do* think it the safest place for firearms; and there they all were — a rifle, a shot-gun, and a brace of revolvers, all in one rack, the first thing you saw when you opened the door. Yet Macturk didn't appear to notice them: he seemed struck of a heap with the extraordinary suitability of my store for his purposes.

"'There's no other door for them to get out by,' says he, rubbing his hands, 'and no windows of any sort. But,' he says, catching hold of my arm in the doorway, 'haven't you a ladder for getting up to those beams and that skylight?'

"'I should have,' said I, 'but it came down with a run under me only last week, and the carpenter's got it to mend.'

"'Capital!' he cried. 'The place might have been made for me.'

"Then he turned to the two of us and explained his game as bold as brass. He was for sticking up this station, as, indeed, we knew already, and he said he'd show us how a station might be stuck up without the least inconvenience to the inhabitants. All the men on the place, except myself, he intended yarding up in the store for the night, which my wife and I were to spend with him in all possible merriment on the right side of the store door. He told us he was fond of music, and that we should find him a man of very simple tastes at the table. At that my wife laughed, as I feared, a little too scornfully. I had visions of a scene, for if Macturk had insulted her — "

"You would have got us all murdered, John, I have no doubt," said Mrs Spurling, filling the pause, from behind her knitting. "But you were wise enough to give your wife's hand a squeeze; and after all she had the sense not to make a fool of herself when it could do no good."

"She had more pluck than the lot of us put together!" exclaimed the squatter, looking from his wife to me with shining eyes. "As I am telling you, there were all those weapons in the rack inside the store, and I felt sure Macturk hadn't spotted them, though they were right in front of our eyes. It gave me palpitations to think of them, for I knew the revolvers were loaded, and I fancied I knew the natures of my men who were to be clapped in there beside them. I didn't think they were the men to be locked up with loaded pistols and not use them the first chance they got; but I'm not so sure about it now. One of them in particular, however— young Pat O'Mara— was a wild Irishman, who could be trusted to do the mad thing in such a case; and I had reasons outside my own skin for wanting no mad doings that night! So I fairly shuddered as I looked out of the tail of my eye at those shooting-irons; and yet it never occurred to me to point them out to Macturk, for it didn't come natural to be tamer with him than was actually necessary. Bless your life, he'd seen them for himself all the time, and I needn't have bothered my head about *that* — for as we were about to leave the store he turned to my wife and pointed to the opposite wall.

"'I must ask you, madam, to be so very kind as to hand me those pretty things from the rack over yonder — for it might prove too strong a temptation to throw in your husband's way,' says he, with a tighter grasp on my arm; 'and even you, my dear madam, I must request to handle them by the barrels only.'

142

"And that was where Mrs Spurling came out so strong, though she sits there and doesn't half like hearing me say so. She took the rifle by the muzzle, in both hands, and passed it over; then the fowling piece; then the revolvers, one in each hand, and I'm hanged if they trembled any more than they do now with those knitting needles! That's my wife, sir! And she and I marched out, arm in arm, with Macturk and all those weapons on our heels, and he made us show him the well next; and in he dropped them, one after the other, and the water splashed above ground after the gun and rifle, the well was so full. Then he stood a bit away from us, and showed us his own revolvers — quite an ordinary brace they were, the most ordinary things about him. It was the first sight we'd had of them, and he only kept them out an instant.

"'They're as much as ever I want,' he said, nodding in the direction of the well; 'but tonight I shan't want any at all. It is quite half-past seven, and it's nearly dark. About time most of your hands were back at the hut, isn't it?'

'About,' said I. 'And here comes one of them,' I added, suddenly descrying a pair of white moleskins through the dark. 'Shall I ask him about the rest?'

"'Certainly.'

"But I saw him feeling for his pistols as the man came up, and he stood just far enough away to watch us as he spoke.

"'Are all you fellows back in the hut yet?'"

"'Yes, sir, all but Pat,' said the man, with his eye on Macturk.

"'And where is Pat?'

"'Can't say; may have gone to the township: you never know where you have Pat.'

"'Well, I want to speak to the lot of you. Will you go back and fetch the others?'

143

"'Stop!' cries Macturk, coming a stride nearer. 'It seems I'm not so ill-known in these parts, but one of your hands knows me. Tell me, my fine fellow, who you think I am ?'

"My man stood and grinned. 'I don't think at all about it, mister,' says he. 'You're our friend Macturk. And I'm proud to set eyes on you at last!'

"'You can't send this man back,' said Macturk. 'You must get the rest some other way.'

"'Not you!' cries my man (who was no favourite with me). 'They'd roll up like lambs to see you, Macturk! We're proud of you in this Colony, my sort are, and we wouldn't touch you if we could, for we know you wouldn't hurt us!'

"I felt inclined to break that man in two, for being so ready to side with the bushranger, so to speak; and to my wife's face too, for she had never left me all this time. But if it came to that, I was siding with the bushranger myself, for I was game to give in to any extent rather than spill blood. After all, too, the man had but spoken a truth which held good pretty well all over the colony in the days of the bushrangers. The best of them never touched a poor man's pocket. They had little to gain by robbing him, but much by making him their friend. They even pandered to him, here and there, by acts of meretricious generosity, that got exaggerated as they spread, and won hearts in a good deal more than half the huts in the Colony. On the other hand, let a man be suspected of betraying their whereabouts, or even of harbouring the police, and they would think nothing of shooting him in cold blood. Thus the greatest difficulty our troopers had to contend with in running these ruffians to earth was the word of the inhabitants, who either did not choose or did not dare to speak the truth. They regarded a popular bushranger with a mixture of terror and hero-worship which held their tongues pretty tight until the man was dead, when they would sing his praises in a way that

144

made you sick. Why, even you may remember how they went on about the Kellys. But Macturk was a greater favourite than ever Ned Kelly was, for he had a far finer manner with him, and a personal magnetism that fascinated you against all your better sense. So I felt tolerably certain that if this man of mine went back to the hut and told his mates who it was that had taken possession of the homestead, they'd roll up, as he said, like lambs. But Macturk himself was less trustful. "'You may mean that, my lad', said he, but I'm worth two hundred pounds, to the man that pots me, and I should be sorry to tempt ye.'

"My man was beautifully indignant.

"'And do you think there's a man of us would touch you for *that*?' he sang out. 'If one of us did, he'd be lynched before ever he saw a note of it, I'll swear to that!' And, indeed, that was pretty much the feeling.

"'You may swear till you're black in the face— there's not a man alive that I'd trust out of my sight,' says Macturk, with one for me in the corner of his eye; and without more ado he took the enthusiast by the arm, and clapped him into my store. He had left us standing in the yard, but we felt his eye was on us all the time, and that his revolver would be too, if we stirred; and for my part I never in my life felt less anxious to show a high spirit. So there we stood, and watched Macturk peep into the kitchen on his way back to us, and purchase our Chinese cook, body and soul, by threatening him with a revolver in each hand. We saw it in the red light of the kitchen, and we laughed, though it was Macturk's one wanton trick that night. In a little he came back to us, and consulted me about getting the other men down from the hut. It ended in our going up there together, and he marched them down in front of him like a mob of sheep; with me at his side feeling a bit of a cur at last;

145

but I had my wife to consider, and it panned out badly enough for us as it was.

"However, the thing was done, and the men weren't hard on me, for they understood well enough. What's more, I'm inclined to think they enjoyed being in the hands of the great Macturk, even to feeling it an honour. In any case they went into that store like children— all except Pat O'Mara, who had never come back. And they behaved like children, and good ones, while there; but I never thought that Pat would have been just the same if he'd been in it too, for he didn't know what fear was, and he had an extraordinary affection for my wife. He is devoted to her to this day. I am anxious about him, by the way, but not half so anxious as I was that night, when I had visions of him turning up at any minute, and showing fight without consulting anybody. Moreover, it was evident that Macturk had him on his mind as well. I heard him questioning the men about him before he locked them up, and afterwards he came to me.

"'See here, Boss,' says. he, 'what sort of a cove's your young friend Pat O'What's-his-name, when he's at home? Which 'twould be a dam' sight better for him if he was now!' he muttered to himself.

"'Pat!' said I, stopping to think; and I decided to tell him like a book. 'He's a young scatter-brain who doesn't know what fear is and for some reasons I wish he was safe in there with the rest, but for some I don't. He'd be sure to show fight before the night was over, if he was there. But the lord knows what he'll do when he turns up and finds out how matters stand!'

"'His blood be on his head,' said Macturk. 'They tell me they think he must have gone to the township. Let's hope, for his skin's sake, that he stays there till morning.'

"I did hope so— with all my heart.

"I must just give you some impression of the night we three had together; then you shall hear what happened after all. It was not quite what I expected of that particular young fellow; but you must hear everything and then judge for yourself.

"We had supper immediately. Our Chinaman cook dished it, and waited on us with his legs shaking under him like drumsticks. He could see, and so could I from the head of the table, that our guest was eating with a revolver lying in his lap, on his napkin; but, from motives of delicacy for which I still like Macturk, the weapon was studiously concealed from my wife, who sat facing the bushranger. Indeed, they talked to one another across the table in a way that made me marvel. My wife shakes her head; but don't you pay any attention to her. I tell you, she was as cool as Macturk himself, and a long chalk cooler then I was, from start to finish.

"After supper was cleared away the Chinkee was shoved into the store among the others, who were sitting about like stuck pigs, all listening hard to anything they could hear through the door, and never dreaming of rebellion. I reckoned we should have found Pat half-way through the skylight, had he been one of them. But Macturk seemed to have forgotten Pat's existence, and now the three of us came out here, and he and I smoked cigars and yarned away like long-lost brothers. That is to say, Macturk did the yarning while we listened; and there's no doubt but what 'twas the most interesting conversation that ever was heard in this verandah. He told us all about the way he stuck up a bank here and a mail-coach there, with once or twice an entire township, to say nothing of stations three times the size of ours; and what had been his best hauls and his narrowest squeaks! There wasn't a clean crime he'd committed but what he told us something about it, as he sat down there on the edge of the verandah and smoked cigars, with one eye on me and the other on the store door. He'd left the dining-room one wide open, with a lamp burning inside, and he was boss of the situation where he sat. Trust him for that: if the store door had been burst open while we were out here he could have sat tight where he was and potted the first man that came through. It was a lovely night, I recollect; with the Southern Cross just over the highest point of the range, and every star like a stab in the crust of hell; but there was no moon. The locusts were chirruping all round the house; they seemed to burst out whenever Macturk made a pause, just as if they were cheering him. Of course they were at it all the time, only we could listen to nothing but his nibs and his yarns. I remember him telling us that he only came to stations when he wanted a new horse or saddle, and that his fancy was to combine pleasure with business on those occasions. And we laughed, because somehow we seemed to have grown quite friendly with the chap, in spite of ourselves; but that was his way. He had the most taking way with him that ever I met with in mortal man: so amusing and so pathetic turn about, with the air of an outcast who should by rights have been a king, and yet so considerate in little things all the time, more particularly in the smallest dealings with Mrs Spurling. It was his way of asking her to play, when we went inside again, that saved him asking twice ; and he sat and listened like a mouse, with his eyes half closed, like the gentleman he was, who'd missed fire the deuce knows how!

"And yet the wary professional side of him was wide awake the whole time. I'll tell you how we knew. My wife had played him two or three soft little things— I could whistle them now, though I forget their names — when Macturk ups and asks for a galop, and she was to play it as loud as ever she knew how. So she gave her piano a proper warming, and at the top of the row Macturk crept up to the store door, made me follow with the lamp — got the wife to bang away louder than ever — flung open the door, and had his revolvers at the men's heads before I had time to guess what it was he was up to. It seemed he had heard a. noise and suspected mischief. But the men were only ragging the unfortunate Chinkee; and resistance was as far from their minds as ever. He threatened them for that, however, telling the Chinkee to sing out the next time he was touched, and he'd shoot the man that dared molest his prisoner, so help him Almighty God. It was a brave bit of swagger, but nothing else; yet it went down even with my wife and me, such was the glamour of the fellow, and there's no denying we thought the more of him when the door was slammed and locked, and all three of us were together once more.

"Well, we had no more music, for by this time it was after midnight (when we looked at the clock), and Macturk himself shut up the piano and thanked Mrs Spurling for the treat she had given him. It was he, too, who wanted her to go off to bed and leave the two of us sitting up; but my wife wouldn't hear of it, for she has always had a notion that when trouble's going her place is by my side, and I've never been able to get this idea out of her head. So there the three of us were stuck, and for a time things hung fire. The yarns had run dry, and Macturk seemed to consider it as much as his life was worth to moisten them with whiskey. So I wouldn't touch any either; but after a bit we brewed some tea, and that cheered us up. Mrs Spurling had forty winks over the fire, and as for me and Macturk, you may think it odd, but we started to play poker. It was his suggestion. So were the points, which were higher than I could afford; but I thought I might as well be robbed this way as another, for of course I never thought of winning and being paid. Yet win I did, and Macturk paid up like a man. He had more ready money on him than I've ever seen in the bush, where you may say that cheques are the only currency of any

149

account; and he lost it all but what he'd stowed away in another pocket and sworn not to touch. So then he offs with his diamond ring, and says how he took it from a coffee-coloured Jew in the Sydney coach, and he spits on it for luck, and rattles it down on the table to plank against all my winnings. I may be a receiver of stolen property, but I've worn that ring ever since."

And the squatter held out his hand, so that the sun hit the ring on his weather-beaten finger and rebounded in spikes of fire. But his eyes were far away in his story.

"How I managed to win, dear knows. It must have been the merest luck, for as I took my last hand, what should I see at the window but Pat's face leering in at us! He looked as white as paper, but there was a murderous light in his eyes that set me on gunpowder for what might happen next moment. I looked at Macturk: he was screwing up his face over his cards; and I was able to give Pat a single shake, that sent his head from the window without being seen. But when the ring was on my finger, and we had shaken hands, I said to Macturk —

"'Get out your shooter: I'm going to the door.'

"I was there before he could answer, but I felt that he was covering me as I stood and called on Pat by his name, imploring him to come in if he was anywhere about. But devil an answer gave Pat, nor could I lay eyes on him in the dark, half blind as I was from the lights of the room. Of course Macturk wanted to know what I'd heard or seen; otherwise he didn't seem in the least disturbed.

"When I'd fairly given it up, I turned round and told him it was a step I'd heard on the verandah.

"'Can you swear to it?' said he.

"'N—no, I can't,' said I, not wanting poor Pat to be unearthed and shot if he raised a finger, as he was pretty safe to do.

150

"'There was no step,' said Macturk. 'I've got the longest ears in the Colony, and I heard nothing at all.'

"So there was an end of the matter; but after that Macturk locked the door and put the key in his pocket, and I pulled down the blind, which had somehow been forgotten, and the clock on the chimney piece struck three.

"The night was dragging through. Between three and four Macturk lay down on the sofa; it was then he told us he slept with one eye open, I'm glad he didn't sleep with it on the door he had just locked. For I saw the handle turning as he lay and dosed, and I knew that it was that young fool Pat trying the door.

"Pat was the trouble! But for him I should have been as easy as my wife, who had no idea he was about. Her only anxiety was Macturk, and he had ceased to be one, be was behaving so prettily. Then, I had won his ring, and evidently I was to stick to it, which would pay for any horse he liked to take in the morning. It was amazing treatment at the hands of a bushranger —hands that had blood on them too, as I have said. But poor Pat! Well, now I'll tell you."

He leant forward in his chair. Mrs Spurling had put down her knitting, and was looking now at her husband, now at me. I scented the end.

"Macturk cut the night shorter than I had dared to hope. At 4.30 he hauled out the Chinkee to cook him his breakfast. Poor devil, he might have known his last hour was come, he ate it so heartily! Then we left the house— the wife still with us— Macturk in the middle. We were going straight to the horse-paddock. Macturk was in great form after his breakfast, apologising to my wife with the grandest air, digging me in the ribs and telling me I hadn't come so badly out of it after all (meaning with his ring), and saying again and again that it was the best night ever he'd put in on a matter of business. Then he gave a sigh at his way of life, and my wife seized the opportunity to put in an earnest word that had been troubling her all the night; and in his gay familiar way— it never struck me to resent it — he ran his arm round her waist, and bent down to thank her. I'll swear it was only to thank her; but next moment he was spread out in the grass, with a bullet in his middle. I gave a look round, and there was the smoke hanging about a little low bush that I'll show you presently, and Pat O'Mara running up to us, trailing an old musket he'd found in the men's hut. He'd a gaping face on him that showed the nerves all newly snapped inside. It seemed he was in doubt after all as to whether he'd done right or wrong. He had been lying in wait half the night.

"My wife was kneeling over Macturk, and I knelt too. But be pushed us aside to get a fair view of the man who had shot him. And never shall I forget the burning scorn in his eyes, nor the withering curl of his lips and nostrils, as he fixed on Pat the look that probably gave the last push to the poor young fellow's reason.

"'You, you!' he said, a mouthful of blood coming up with the words. 'You might have given me a show!'

"He was dead, but I was listening at his heart, when there was a click behind me; and there was Pat cocking his musket and pointing it at his own head. I struck at the barrel, and the bullet he had just slipped in passed through the brim of his wideawake."

Mr Spurling stood up and stretched himself.

"Faith," said he, "it's almost a pity I struck so soon! The man has never been like other people from that day to this. The countryside would give him no peace about it. Macturk haunted him too; so the thing hit from within and from without. We had to get him police protection for a time; but poor chap, all the police in Christendom couldn't protect him from himself. He went off his head by fits and starts; he isn't wholly off it now. He isn't much good to me, but I couldn't turn him away. After all, he only did what was right and proper: but he was made to think otherwise, and Heaven knows what effect your likeness to Macturk has had upon him. Shall we go and look for him now? And I'll show you the place where it all happened; it's behind the house."

We found the poor wretch cowering in the scrub. He fell on his knees to me, and, with the tears running down his cheeks, asked me to forgive him. It was at last brought home to him that I was not Macturk. And we left him tootling on a penny whistle, which, it appeared, was his safety -valve whenever his emotions proved too much for him.

"For doing his duty!" I said, as we walked back to the homestead. "Surely in the long run you saw that it was the proper thing to do, and were grateful to this poor fellow, rather than otherwise?"

"I can never be that," said my host sadly. "His shot killed two lives: our only child was born— and died— that day. As for Macturk, there is no doubt that Pat performed a public service in shooting him like a dog. He only got his deserts, after all. And, mind you, though the glamour of the fellow was a kind of spell over my wife and me the night we had him here, there was a great lot of humbug about him when all is told. See this ring? I wear it in memory of a celebrated scoundrel. But it is no more a diamond than I am."

A Lochinvar of the
Old Man Plain

Joe Callaghan was "knocking down his cheque".

There are two ways of performing this feat. You may strut into the shanty and toss it across the bar, with appropriate bravado, and the request that they will tell you when you have got to the bottom of that. This is the traditional and picturesque method. The other way is to be decoyed into that shanty against a whole year's resolutions; to let them have your cheque "to take care of", when you are no longer capable of doing so yourself, or of appreciating the transaction at all; and remain in this condition until they choose to turn you out penniless, too ill to argue, too weak to resist, despoiled of a twelve months' earnings in the inside of a week. The latter, unhappily, is the commoner, more inglorious, and most iniquitous way of it. And it was the way of Joe Callaghan, among a hundred thousand others.

Joseph had no intention of drawing rein at Scarlett's Hotel on the Old Man Plain: the lonely hostelry was too like others which had more than once been the ruin of him a couple of hundred miles further back. But then there had been the excuse of sore feet, a heavy swag, and the comparatively small cheque of the pound-a-week stockman; whereas now he was a prosperous young shearer, with a good mare under him, which had carried him unscathed through Ivanhoe, Mossgiel, Booligal, and Hay itself. To play the fool within fifty miles of Deniliquin and the rail, and a day's journey of the old folk "down in Vic.", was the last thing that Joseph dreamt of doing. But he was ahead of his time; there was no train till eight o'clock in the morning; he would "strike" Deniliquin in the middle of the night. And Scarlett's Hotel lay in the palm of the great round plain, so cool and cleanly in the moonshine, with laughter and lamps and even music across the Rubicon of the wide verandah.

Even dance music, which a man must hum as he rode; it was struck up as Joseph ambled into earshot; and he walked his horse to keep the time.

"Here comes a shearer," Dan Scarlett had cried. "Look alive, Diner! Down you sit! Bang away! If you let him pass, my word, you'll be sorry for it! Keep it up — faster — louder — that's the style!"

And the old reprobate performed a *pas seul* behind the door, with his cabbage-tree hat on the back of his head, and his noble beard waggling upon his red shirt, until every glass and bottle in the adjoining bar rang its own chime, and the jingle of a spur outside announced that the fly was in the outer meshes of the web.

The subsequent stages would make ugly reading. This particular spider had reduced the whole proceeding to a science, but it was only in his opening move that he was original. He never asked any man in, so he never frightened any man away; he trusted to music and sounds of merriment, and was shrewd enough to see that such attractions are the stronger to the uninvited. Once he had his man, Scarlett relied upon his daughter to keep him; he had her educated for the infamous part; with what success you may gather from the fate of Joseph Callaghan .

It was about nine in the evening when curiosity compelled this unhappy young man to see what was going on inside,. By then he was dancing with Dan himself in the verandah, a grotesque performance, to which the daughter thumped within, while the shearer's mare eyed him sadly from the outer

155

darkness, her reins still on the hook where they had been flung for five minutes. Midnight saw the animal comfortably at large in the horse-paddock, and her master sleeping in his spurs on a bench outside the bar.

He had not moved at dawn, when the place was once more in a bustle. The Deniliquin coach was in sight; the five fresh horses had just been run up; and Dinah was yawing in her glass, and extracting the curling pins from her frizzy hair, because Dan Scarlett would have her preside at the half-crown breakfast, which yielded two shillings clear profit per head.

"Diner," cried the publican, who was beaming upon the prostrate shearer when the girl emerged blinking. "Diner, you take one end and we'll have him out o' this for the meantime. We don't want the poor devil woke up just yet a bit. Catch hold of that end. Steady does it. So!"

And the bench was dragged and jolted to the far end of a side verandah, without disturbing a feature of the sleeper's face. His head went from side to side, an arm fell, the knuckles trailed; but not an eyelid moved, and Dan's smile broadened as he loosed his hold and stood upright.

"Wait a bit, Diner!" said he, as the girl was going with the same evil grace with which she had lent her aid, "I've got a word to say to you, my lass. You see our friend here? Well, you've got to keep him like that all day."

"Me?" cried Dinah, her eyes dilating. "Shan't you be here then?"

"No. I'm going as far as Schneider's with the coach, and I'll be back by the down coach this evening. Schneider's got a buggy and pair he wants to sell, and I might do a deal after this." He jerked his head towards the bench, and winked. "A three-figure cheque!" he whispered. "Three blooming figures! I have it safe in the cash box; but don't you ever let him get

156

within coo-ee of asking for it; pour the stuff down his throat as soon as he offers to open his mouth."

"And am I to sit down and watch him all day?" asked Dinah in disgust.

"You've got to do as I tell yer," snarled Dan. "You can do it the way you think best; but let me find that josser on his legs when I come back, and I'll knock you off yours, so sure as God made sour apples!!

His white beard splayed as he wagged his head; his red nose shone in the first flush of the rising sun; and at breakfast that morning Dinah Scarlett was not herself. Booligal Bob, the smartest coachman on the route, whose driving-coat was never without a flower, which of late he had invariably presented to Dinah, was quite concerned about her as he flicked his three leaders and drove away.

"Kinder lonely life for a gal," said he to Dan; and he readjusted the wideawake with which he had waved farewell to the solitary little figure in the wide verandah.

"She ain't lonely," was Dan's reply. "She don't have time. An astonishing comfort to me, that lassie," he added, fondly; and Booligal Bob sighed in sympathy.

Nevertheless, though Dinah Scarlett was probably the loneliest mortal on the Old Man Plain, she would still have given a good deal that morning to have felt lonelier still; the occupant of the side verandah was on her nerves as well as on her hands for the day. Not that she had conceived the smallest sentimental interest in his case. It is true that to Dinah such exhibitions were too common a spectacle to be very shocking in themselves; similarly, the girl was too used to her father's and her own hand in them to have a proper shame for either. To be brought up in an atmosphere of debauchery on the proceeds of extortion is to regard such matters in a light of one's own. Yet Dinah Scarlett was not without refinement of a kind, nor the complementary quantum of self-respect. She wore vivid frocks, which, nevertheless, suited her sunburnt complexion and her very black hair, and she could play dance music with considerable spirit and velocity. Dan had sent her to the school in Deniligin for the sole purpose of acquiring this accomplishment; if she had come back slightly superior to her lot, the superiority did not include a sudden horror of scenes to which she had been accustomed from the cradle. But what she remembered of Joseph overnight, and what she had seen of him that morning, were equally unattractive and undesirable in eyes which Dinah had perhaps endowed with a certain rudimentary fastidiousness. Dinah started the day, in short, with no personal pity or consideration for the sleeping hog on the side verandah, but she resented the sordid duty which had been thrust upon her; and, above all, she dreaded the consequences if she failed in its fulfilment.

What if the brute jumped up and demanded his cheque? Her instructions were to keep him unfit to do anything of the sort; but what if she failed! She would find herself between two brutes, a helpless girl; for Ada, the strapping bar-maid, was no friend of Dinah's, and Billy Hall, the potman and general rouseabout, had already gone to turn out the coach-horses, and was going on to the station for killing sheep, an all-day job; nor was there another soul about the premises but Sammy, the Chinese cook.

So Dinah reflected as she remade the toilet which had been scamped perforce in the smaller hours. And she looked dainty and pretty enough when she reappeared in the hot verandah, and not really vulgar after all; for her pert face lacked its usual assurance, and a general air of trouble and anxiety made for modesty and repose.

It was within a week of Christmas and the fever of the earth was at its height. Brown and bare it lay from lip to lip of the great inverted bowl of blue — blue with a single break through which intolerable light and heat poured without ceasing all day long. Every now and then the iron roof crackled like distant musketry. Shadows were short and sharp; and beyond them the baked earth swam and trembled in the heat. No other habitation was visible from this one; no traveller loomed on the horizon. The barmaid was invisible and probably asleep. Sammy's slippers trailed and flopped lazily in the kitchen across the yard; and in the side verandah the besotted shearer still slumbered on his back. Dinah stole a look at him on the points of her high-heeled shoes. His position was the same but he had kicked off one of his spurs, his wideawake had also fallen, and Dinah noted the length of the one and the blue silk fly-veil that was the other. Now a fly-veil is one of the three or four unmistakable signs of a bush dandy; long spurs are another; and both appealed to Dinah as she crept away in her own exceedingly smart bronze shoes.

What a mercy there was no mosquitoes and next to no flies! It was too hot for either; wherefore, as it was evidently not too hot for him, there was no reason why the man on the verandah should not sleep all day. Yet it could hardly be the quantity he had drunk, and Dinah was reminded of a violent scene caused by a squatter who had once driven up and accused her father of drugging the drinks and poisoning his men. She wondered if the drinks had been drugged last night; if so she was sorry for that poor shearer. And she hated her father for meddling with his cheque; but for that there would have been nothing to dread in the return to his senses of a young man who wore a blue fly-veil and long spurs.

The coolest room was the one adjoining the bar; where there was little furniture but the piano that had been part of the investment which had included Dinah's sojourn at Deniligin. Hither came Dinah in the end to while away the time at her piano; but first she shut all the doors behind her, and one bronze shoe was firmly planted on the soft pedal as a further precaution. Then Dinah looked through her music, and none of it pleased her at all. She was sick of waltzes, and they required an audience; and at the school she had been made to fly so much higher; here was one of the pieces at the bottom of the stack — a piece by a man of the name of Chopin, which had no tune at all so far as Dinah could make out, but ant any rate it was something to do, and at it she went accordingly. In the same spirit and with equal tenacity she would have welcomed and wrestled with any other purely manual task; for Dinah had plenty of determination, as any listener that morning might have learnt for his sins. And on floundered Dinah for nearly twenty minutes — killing time and slowly torturing a classic — until the warm keys were as damp as her face and fingers, and the deed was done.

Yet no groans came through the weather-board walls; no thanks went up to heaven that all was over; the place was as still as ever, the verandah as empty, the horizon as barren, when Dinah emerged and drank deep from the hanging waterbag.

There were still no signs of the independent Ada or of the meal which would turn the endless morning into finite afternoon. Dinah still had everything all to herself — Dinah and her bugbear in the side verandah. Would he never wake up? Much as she feared him she began to wish he would; anything would be better than this intolerable loneliness and nervous apprehension; but she would take one more peep.

She took it on tiptoe as before.

The man was gone.

Gone also were the long spur and the wideawake with the silk fly-veil; gone all three from the flimsy weather-board premises notorious as Scarlett's Hotel!

No doubt Callaghan had been duly drugged; it is incredible that a sound young fellow would have gone into a twelve-hours' torpor as the net result of two or three of careless indiscretion rather than of wilful excess. And Scarlett's reputation is still remembered in the matter of drugs. But in this instance he would have done better to devote more time and less labelled poison to his atrocious task. As the sequel may show.

Joseph began life again by wondering why his bed was so hard; he turned over and met the floor simultaneously with shoulder, ribs and thigh. He sat up, and clapped both hands to his head to hold it on. It contained an aching chaos instead of yesterday's brains. Joseph would have paid anybody handsomely to tell him who and where he was. Those whitewashed verandah posts were insolently new to him. He had never seen that horse-yard or those outbuildings before. And the place was painfully — abnormally — insufferably still.

He got to his feet and was glad to sit down again where he had lain so long. He reached his hat and examined it thoughtfully before putting it on; he retrieved his spur, and examined that. Neither suggested any clue, and again he listened. Slippers pothered in the distance; the roof crackled overhead; and the listener's ears sang their own song, a song he knew only too well, that told him he had been making a fool of himself again. Instinctively his hand slid into one of the cross-pockets of his moleskins. It encountered coins, and Joseph smirked as he nodded to himself. Things might be worse. Moreover, he began to remember; and now a faint wild war with a pianoforte added itself gradually to the other sounds; and next instant he had remembered nearly all.

Again he found his feet, and this time plunged into an adventurous circuit of the verandah, in which the whitewashed posts proved good friends to him, and the hanging waterbag a better still. How grateful was the wholesome flavour of canvas in the pure cold fluid! It became easier and easier to stand upright; and now Joseph realised that the music was very near to him, and he wondered whether it would sound such a jumble to sober ears. With a face full of cunning he crept to a door of which the upper panels were glass. And through this he stood and gazed.

The piano cut off a corner of the room, and Dinah presented more back than profile to the glass door as she sat on the music-stool and made the noonday hideous. But the bushman's ear was not sensitive, and for what it suffered his eyes repaid him. Dinah was in her usual cool attire splashed with vivid hues. She put Joseph in mind of a sheaf of pale corn bound with scarlet, and in the cool dusk of the sheltered room the effect quite transported the unsteady young man. It was his turn to stand on tiptoe as he felt for the handle, and his heavy eyes were awake and alight with mischief when all at once they saw themselves and more in the bad glass of the door.

It may have been the inferior quality of the mirror, or of Joseph's vision that morning, or both; but a more distorted, bloated, unshaven and unlovely countenance he had never encountered; and he was really rather a good looking young man. He fell back in time, shocked, humiliated and abashed. And so it was that the murderous music proceeded without interruption to its abominable end.

Meanwhile Joseph had sought his mare and found his saddle, bridle and valise; but with these he was scouring the horse-paddock, with the fixed intention of riding straight away, when the money in his pocket and the mud on his brain reminded him of preliminary obligations; and having caught

162

the mare he sat down to think. He liked the look of that girl. And he owed her something for tempting him in last night. But he did not like the look of himself as he remembered it in that glass door. He must pull himself together if he was to take much change out of a smart little devil like that; and as he sat and looked about him, he saw the way.

A table of sand rose between him and the horse-paddock fence and the hotel beyond; that table was the lip of a tank; and in that tank Mr Callaghan was floundering what time poor Dinah searched the house for him in vain.

"Do I know where he is?" echoed Ada, disturbed in her siesta, and by consequence ruder than usual to her particular foe. "Not likely! What do you take me for? Do your own dirty work. Keep an eye on your own fancy; that's my advice."

"He's not my fancy!" exclaimed Dinah, heaving with indignation and distress.

"No? Well, he's your look out, whether or no. It's you that's got to keep 'im paralytic — not me. It's you that'll hear about it if he's given us the slip!"

Dinah understood the special venom of the other's triumph. She said no more, but went to Sammy in his kitchen.

"Me know!" cried the Chinaman instantly. "Wellee drunk last night — all lite now. Gone catchee horsee longa horse-paddock."

"Gone to catch his horse, has he?" said Dinah, with momentary relief. Then she raised her hand and peered under it towards the horse-paddock fence and beyond but saw no sign of horse or horseman; for the banked-up sides of the tank looked low enough at half-a-mile, but at that moment they hid both man and beast.

Without further question, Dinah ran into the harness-room, and, of course, the shearer's trappings had vanished like himself. He could not have been asleep at all when she peeped at him that last time. He must have caught his mount with the least possible loss of time and ridden off like the wind. A slight sandy acclivity brought the southern horizon comparatively close, and Dinah pictured him already on its further slope.

"Did he come back to saddle up?" She returned to inquire in the kitchen, when she had scanned the blinding plain once more.

Sammy grinned.

"No, missee. Him plenty stlong debble. Takee sadlee — blidelee — whole bag o'tlicks!"

Dinah went back to the house, and a grim interest in the upshot supplanted her first despair. The shearer's cheque had been taken from him, and, having discovered his loss, he had galloped off without a word. That looked ominous. Dinah foresaw his return in stern company; and she tried to foresee her life if her father were put in prison and this sequestered sink of dishonesty and intemperance should cease to be her home. The prospect might have filled her with a livelier filial anxiety but for its alternative if the publican were the first to reappear. As it was, Dinah could contemplate the worst with an equanimity which became positive satisfaction when Ada flounced into the room to fling the cloth on the table and the knives and forks upon the cloth.

"No signs of him yet," said she. "I'm sorry for you Miss Dinah, my word!"

"You may be sorry yourself before you're done," was Dinah's mysterious retort.

"May I, then? I should like to know what it's got to do with me. The job wasn't given to me. I ain't the landlady."

"And I don't think you ever will be," said Dinah quietly; after which she was allowed to sit down in peace, so far as her enemy was concerned. But, as she was still wrestling with the

164

cold mutton and the baking-powder bread, though spending more time over the *Australasian,* and still more upon her own reflections, the knife and fork dropped suddenly on her plate. A pair of spurs were trailing along the verandah.

"Am I too late for a feed?" inquired a jovial voice, and a blue fly-veil fluttered in the doorway as the shearer's hat was taken off with just such a flourish as Dinah would have expected of him. Yet she could hardly recognise the ignoble tenant of the side verandah. His shirt and moleskins were of dazzling cleanliness. He had knotted a gay silk handkerchief about his sunburnt throat. He had even contrived to shave without wounding himself severely. In short, under cover of the horse-paddock tank, Joseph Callagan had improved himself by various little alterations which he had intended making at Deniliquin; and a smart, upstanding and decidedly good-looking young bushman was the product.

"No you're just in time," was what Dinah said, as she pushed back her chair. What she felt was consternation aggravated by suspense. Had he come back for his cheque? No, he looked much too amiable; but he was also palpably and incredibly sober; and the one other thing of which Dinah felt certain was that she herself was in for a bad time first or last.

"Don't get up," said Joseph, as she rose.

"But I'm finished."

"I thought you said I was in time?" he grumbled, gallantly.

"So you are; I will go an order it when you let me pass."

"I won't look at it unless you come back and see me through!"

"Very well."

He stood aside; but now she hesitated.

"What — what will you take to drink?" she faltered.

"What do you recommend?" said he, slyly.

165

What could she recommend? Dinah despised herself much, but she feared her father more, and, "The whiskey s ver y good, they say", she answered in such a transparent little tone that it was all the gay Joseph could do to keep from snatching her off her feet and kissing her then and there. Instead, he shook his head in humorous reproof, and Dinah smirked and blushed, but could have cried for shame.

"It isn't nice of you to mention whiskey," said Joe. "I don't call it altogether kind. Accidents will happen when a cove's been up the bush twelve months on end, but I'm sure you ain't the one to want to make 'em worse; you wouldn't have me stop and knock down my cheque, would you? No, Miss, no more of your whiskey for me; it didn't taste quite the clean potato, not to me it didn't; but we'll say no more about that. Give me a good hot pannikin of tea — and come back and help me drink it before I clear."

The tea was made and presently consumed, together with a healthy portion of the cold mutton and the baking powder bread, the table cleared with silent scorn by Dinah's enemy, but her friend from the back-blocks betrayed no immediate anxiety to "clear" in his turn. In fact, he had engaged that young woman in a flirtation, of which it is happily unnecessary to give a realistic report. Refinement is not the note of up-country inns or of back-block woolsheds; and where the orgy of the night before was a fruitful topic of recriminatory badinage, the mere delicacy of the conversation was necessarily not its strong point. It was none the less above the average of its kind, thanks to Deniliquin in the one case and certain racial characteristics in the other. Mr Callaghan had been born in the bush without a brogue; but he had inherited full measure of the sunny temperament and the light touch of his forefathers, and both made their mark on Dinah's susceptibilities. She forgot her father and the wrath to come; she forgot Ada in the bar next

166

door; and her eyes grew so bright as she sat on the music-stool, now whirling her back on Joseph and playing a half-hearted bar, now turning to shake her head at him on that convenient swivel; and her cheek grew such a charming reddish brown at his bolder sallies, that the insinuating Joseph began to forget things too.   It was quite a shock to him to remember that he was only there to "take some change" out of the siren who had played him into that den the night before; he was reminded of it in the midst of a glowing description of the old folks' selection down in "Vic.", whither he was bound.

"Ah," said Dinah, over her shoulder; "there'll be a girl down in Vic., I know!"

As it happened there was not; but Joseph, reminded of his revenge, made the requisite admission with a reluctance which carried conviction in every hesitating syllable; whereupon Dinah, revolving on her stool in a glow of jealousy, insisted on knowing what the other girl was like, and so fired a mine of falsehood for her own mystification.   "The girl in Vic." seemed to be everything that Dinah was not but would have been if she could; there was downright cruelty in Joseph's description of her stately height and golden hair, and his convincing "My word"!" after each new invention put a barb on every point.

Dinah, however, feigned the most unselfish interest, and wanted to know when they were going to be married.   Joseph said he thought next week; or perhaps the week after; it was what he was going "down to Vic. for", at any rate; and it was the reason why he mustn't knock his cheque down this time, for it represented his capital for married life.   At this Dinah whisked round on her stool, and played more bars than she had done yet during the afternoon, and showed a redder ear and cheek.   And in a sudden flash Joe Callaghan remembered.

Till this moment the safety of the small money in his pocket had seemed a vague guarantee for that of the big cheque in his pouch. At all events, with the former to pay his way out, Joseph had not troubled about the latter; but now he remembered something that sent both his hands to his pouch, It was but a word or two, a wheedling voice, a white beard, an outstretched palm, rescued from the oblivion of his drunkenness, but it was enough.

"Where's the boss?"

His voice was rough and loud. Dinah turned round and then rose, because he had risen first. His face filled her with fear and shame.

"He went up to Schneider's by the coach."

"When will he be back?"

"By the coach this evening."

"Thank you; that'll do," said Joseph, sternly. He swung on his heel but was overtaken at the door, and compelled to shake a small hand from his arm.

"Whatever's the matter?" Dinah could not help crying, though she knew so well. "Is it your cheque?"

"Yes; where is it? It's been taken from me. I've been robbed of my money. I'll have it back, or ther'll be trouble in the camp!"

"You haven't been robbed of it," said Dinah, doggedly. "You gave it to my father to take care of it for you. I saw you do it."

"It was the same thing," returned the young man, furiously. "I didn't know what I was doing. I've seen that old game played before: drug him first and rob him after. But it's not going to come off this time. If he's only taking care of it, he can give it me back; and if you know where it is you can save me the trouble and prevent a barney you won't forget."

"But I don't," cried Dinah, losing her head and trying to establish her innocence. "I know nothing about it. You shouldn't be angry with me when it wasn't my fault."

"Oh no," he sneered. "We're very innocent, ain't we? We weren't chartered to keep a chap tight all day? We didn't do our part last night, I suppose, from the very start? Bah! I know all about you; like father, like daughter. But it won't come off this time — not much!"

And he strode into the verandah, slamming the glass door behind him, so that every pane rattled and rang again.

The hot sun set quickly in a clean-edged crimson ball that seemed to rest a few minutes on the edge of the world before rolling over into space. For those few minutes the glass doors of Scarlett's Hotel were panelled with flaming gold, and there was a vivid glint to every bottle in the bar; a few more and the ball of blue was a bowl of purple, pricked with a new star every instant, and filled already with the balmy cool of the sub-tropical night. But a horse that had been tethered to the verandah-post in broad daylight stood there still, and in the road an upright figure paced as steadily under the stars as in the light of the sun; and Dinah watched him put a fresh match to his pipe from time to time, and wrung her hands as the flame lit his handsome, angry, determined face.

Whatever became of his anger and determination, her guerdon would be the same; but it was not this sure prospect which gave Dinah her most poignant emotions. It would be time enough to cry when she was hurt; what troubled her most meanwhile was that the aggrieved young man in the road would think her as bad as her father. She wished him to think better of her before he went. She had an altogether unreasonable longing for his good opinion, for which she refused to account even to herself, and which she made no real effort to conquer. He would go "down to Vic." thinking everything that was mean of her; he would tell the lanky horror with the dyed hair — so ran her thoughts, in circles of mortification and regret, until her head swam. She could tell Dyed Hair something, too. She could tell her of the long afternoon she had with Mr Callaghan before he missed his cheque. Oh, if he had not missed it so soon! If she could only show him still that she, at any rate, was not so low and mean as he thought her! If she could but think of some way!

And think of one she did — at the eleventh hour. But — dare she do it? Had she the courage? And as she asked herself these questions, Mr Callaghan had stood still: two red eyes had appeared on the northern horizon: the coach was in sight.

Joseph had resumed his walk when the bronze shoes pattered in the road, and he turned round to see Dinah standing in the starlight, with a slip of paper fluttering from an outstretched, trembling hand.

"Here it is, Joe!"

He took it and held it to his eyes.

"So you knew where it was, eh?"

"Yes, in the cash-box — but I didn't put it there; I didn't, indeed!"

He looked at her as closely as was possible by the light of mere stars. It necessitated a reduction of the feet between them by two inches. And then she seemed so frightened, so troubled, so bent on flight, that Joseph's arm shot suddenly into a position that would have been more becoming in a ballroom than under the windows of Scarlett's Hotel.

"And why couldn't you give it me at once?" said he. "Why were you such a little goose?"

"I hadn't the key."

"Then how did you get it now?"

"I broke open the box."

Joseph followed her eyes. Those of the coach were growing brighter and larger and wider apart with every moment. The girl was watching them with a fixed expression.

"What made you go and do that?" asked the shearer.

"Because it wasn't my fault — and you thought it was — and I didn't want you to go away thinking so — because it wasn't!" cried Dinah again, turning her head to hide her tears.

Joseph drew her nearer.

"But won't you get into trouble for breaking open the cash-box?" said he.

"Trouble!" cried the girl. "There'll be trouble enough in any case; that won't make much difference. I was left to look after you — to keep you on the broad of your back all day! There — it's out. But I shall hear about it, my word! The cash-box won't make it much worse; but never you mind me; it'll all be the same in a hundred years. Give me a sovereign for what you've had, and away you go; only, don't you go and tell the girl in Vic. I tried to rob you of your cheque!"

Joseph drew her nearer still.

"There's no girl in Vic.," he whispered; "no, I take my colonial oath there isn't — and if there was, I'd see her to blazes! Listen to me. There's the coach, and you've got to make up your mind quick. I'm not going to leave you here to pay the shot, so which is it to be? Shall I stay or will you come with me straightaway?"

"Come with you?" gasped Dinah. "How? Where to?"

"On my horse — down to Deniligin - down to Vic. There's no girl there, but there's going to be: the old folk — they want it. Will you take the bullet?"

Dinah's answer was inaudible in the verandah, where an unseen witness crouched in the least light. It didn't prevent Joseph from drawing her gently to where the mare stood tethered, nor yet from swinging her into his saddle, and

171

galloping south with Dinah just as the cracking of the coachman's whip came into earshot of Scarlett's Hotel.

Passengers for Deniligin had to fend for themselves that night at Scarlett's on the Old Man Plain. They had brought their host home the worse for wear from his friend Schneider's hospitality, and they heard him seeking his daughter with threats and imprecations while they made their hurried meal. They left him uncorking a new demijohn, closely attended by a strapping young woman, who smiled to herself when he shouted out that he would overtake them inside of five miles. They had seen nothing of him when daylight found them breakfasting at the Pretty Pine, and those who took train at Deniligin were struck by the figure of a fine young bushman with long spurs and a blue fly-veil, who stood to the last on guard over a first-class compartment with an ominous legend stuck across the window.

The Best of the Bushrangers

Admittedly they were a very bad lot indeed, to be the best of whom was to remain a double-dyed villain after all. There is, however, abundant evidence that Henry Power, alias Henry Johnston, the really gallant ruffian who, under arms, robbed one hundred and fourteen persons (but never a woman) without killing one, was something more than the boldest and yet least bloodthirsty of Australian bushrangers. There was more transparent good in him than the world has usually discovered in its great criminals, and a vast deal more than will transpire in the following anecdote, which is no petty fable of sinner turned saint. It is, on the other hand, one of the many yarns current in the Colony of Victoria, and more or less illustrative of the fine audacity, rough-and-ready chivalry and grim humour of Power. Nor can I recall having ever seen it in print; nor yet vouch for its historical truth. I can but tell the tale as it was told to me, over a blazing camp-fire, within a few furlongs of its alleged scene.

The affair began as a professional incident of the almost every-day routine. It appears that Power was short of money, and of other sinews of the guerrilla warfare which it was his pleasure to wage against mankind. He had therefore descended from his fastness among the ranges (that despair of the police), and put himself in ambush at a point where it descended through thick timber to a creek, to rise very abruptly on the opposite side. It was in the bed of this creek, which was dry, that Power hid, watching for the coach, but wistfully desiring the earlier apparition of easier prey.

There were two sides to sticking up a coach. You got more out of it, but you ran very much greater risks. Among half-a-

173

dozen male passengers there was too strong a chance of at least one set of nerves and one stock of courage to equal those of the bushranger. Once, to be sure, he had held up a coach containing no fewer than sixteen passengers, many of them men, who had nevertheless offered him no sort of resistance. But that was an experience which Power hardly expected to repeat.

Judge therefore of his joy when a single horseman appeared a good hour before any coach was due. The outlaw's first act was to spring upon his horse, by whose side its considerate master had been standing in the dry bed of the creek; he badly needed a better mount, and at a glance he made sure of that at least. The approaching rider came thundering down the gentler slope at a headlong pace which argued the sure foot and the sound knees which were Power's primary requirements, and he had to put spurs to his own worn steed in order to intercept his victim. This he did with his rifle in rest, and the confident air and jovial voice of he determined ruffian who has seldom met with opposition.

But for once Power had trouble with his man, whose behaviour was aggravated by his youth. In an instant this intrepid young man had dragged his horse almost upon its haunches, so that sparks flew from its slithering hind hoofs, while a revolver spat quickly but wildly, as it were between the animal's ears. The bushranger, sitting uninjured, seemed too amazed to return the fire, and is said to have owned that he was only aroused when the empty pistol was hurled after the last shot, with no better aim, and the infuriated rider dashed at a tangent into the thick timber on the right-hand side of the track.

The chase that followed was short and sharp enough, yet it carried the couple well back from the road, and it finished in a glade green with ferns and open to the downpour of a vertical sun. The young man's horse had stumbled, emptying the young man over its head; but he was up again in an instant, his white face working in the strong light. And it would seem to have been the more desperate face of the two; though covered now by a long barrel, held with muscles of iron against a shoulder like solid rock.

"Throw up those hands, sonny, or you're dead boy."

"I don't care!"

And the fool made a suicidal effort to fling himself into his saddle, whereupon Power, spurring closer with an oath, rapped him smartly across the head with his rifle barrel.

"There! I've let you off for the last time. Up with those hands like Winky, or I'll drill a hole through you without more blarney."

There was no help for it, and this time the youth obeyed, though with bitter grace, and eyes wild with hatred for his panting horse. It was the better one of the two; the chase had proved it; but for that stumble, he would have got away. His heart seemed broken by his failure to do so; his jaw fell, his lips trembled. It was as though he stood confronted with instant death. Power had seen the look before, and he hastened to give explicit re-assurance on the point.

"I'm not a-going to shoot you now, my boy," said he, "not unless you try them games again. Do you know who I am? I'm Harry Power. Did you never hear of me before?"

"Oh, I've heard of you," said the young man, gloomily, "and I knew who you were from the first. I've seen you in the waxworks."

There was, indeed, no mistaking the firm, square shoulders, the snuff-coloured beard, and the piercing black eyes of Henry Power. He was not only the typical bushranger of his generation, he was the very prince of his type. And yet the mere mention of the waxworks set him grinning through his virile beard.

175

"Then why did you want to make me go and plug you, my lad? You know, or ought to know, that I never did such a thing in the whole course of my career."

The youth was not listening; he was peering down towards the road (which lay deep in a timbered basin of the ranges), though with little of the eagerness that might have been looked for in a captive. The outlaw's grin turned none the less quickly to a frown; his vanity was piqued, his suspicions aroused, and he continued frowning through some minutes of heavy thought.

"I've told you my name," he at last exclaimed, sternly. "Suppose you take the trouble to look this way and tell me yours?"

"John Smith," was the prompt reply, made, however, with an insolent disregard of the preliminary command.

"Your real name!" cried the bushranger, turning brown in the face. "And you look at me, you jackanapes. Or by heaven I'll make you!"

Whereupon the young man complied but as one who heard the summons for the first time and did not hear the threats at all. On the contrary, he took the formidable Power at rather better than his word and not only looked at him, but through and through him in his turn.

"All right," he said at length; "after all, it can't do any real harm. My name is John, but I don't mind admitting it isn't Smith. It's Jack Falcon, since you so particularly want to know."

"And not a bad name for you, either," said Power, regaining his good nature with the point; "for there's more than a bit of the hawk about you, if you ask me. But see here, sonny, if you're a hawk I'm a darned great eagle; and you stuff that into your pipe! You're too cool and stiff with me, my lad; look out I don't leave you a bit cooler and stiffer still."

176

And the outlaw tapped his piece with a grim humour; but the other twitched shoulders with a wry smile and an involuntary glance towards the road.

"I'm less cool than you think," said he.

"What's the good of looking down there?"

"It's the road, you know," said Falcon, suggestively. But he had the sense to turn his back upon it.

"Well? What then? Do you think I'm going to let you hail the coach, or anybody else that comes along?"

"I don't suppose you are."

"I don't suppose I am," echoed the bushranger, dryly, " so you may as well make the best of it, and turn those pockets of yours inside out. Quick's the word, and don't you miss any! I've got to see the linin' of all the lot."

Pale as he had been before, young Falcon turned paler yet at this explicit command. His fingers fumbled at the pockets, as if to gain time; they did no more, for the other's great eye was upon him all the time.

"Stop a bit," said Power, displaying unexpected patience. "Where do you come from, eh? No lies this time; you may as well spit it out first as last."

"Euroa then," said Falcon sullenly.

Power's face lighted up.

"Aha!" said he. "And you're on your way down to Melbourne, are you?"

"I was, but I've given that up."

"Then you're a young fool," said Power, testily. "Don't you know me by hearsay better than that? Are you such a blessed new chum that you've never heard tell o' me before? I may be a bad lot, but I'm not one of the worst. I may take the lion's share, but darn my skin if I ever took all! No, no; you'll have to part with that horse and saddle of yours, but you'll find mine'll take you down to Melbourne all right, though you

177

won't have to go quite so fast as you were going just now. And I'm not going to take your last stiver; you shall keep enough for drinks along the road. So you look alive and let me see the colour of your coin."

Falcon, however, must renew his fumbling; and Power had to cock his rifle with a horrid click and still worse oaths before the young fool would obey. By this time the latter had shown his hand; and it was a very fine hand of bank-notes, extracted at last, and with piteous reluctance, from an inner pocket. But it was not fine enough for the wily Power, who shook his head over the counted notes.

"No, no, my son ; you don't ride like that for fifty pounds, nor yet look a rifle in the muzzle as you've been looking into mine; not to speak of the way you let loose with your own little iron to start with. You don't do all that for fifty pounds. So where's the rest of it? That's what I want to get at!"

"The rest! Isn't fifty pounds enough for you?"

"It might be if it was the lot."

"I tell you it is!"

"Your tongue may," said Power, "but your face and your voice are singing another tune. You've acted your part very pretty, makin' all them bones about fifty pounds, but you've got to act better than that to do old Power in the weather eye. I want the rest — that's what I want, and if there's enough of it I don't say but what you mayn't get your fifty quid back again. I never clean a man right out if I can help it. But I've got to see what there is, so now you know it. Either you fork out straight or I strip you inch by inch to the skin."

Falcon held his tongue; his face was half-sulks and half-defiance. He was still acting badly.

"Right you are," said Power. "It's all one to me. Suppose you begin by pulling off those precious fine riding-boots?"

And the acting ceased upon the word.

178

The noonday sun, pouring yet more vertically into that oasis of green ferns amid a forest of tall and sombre trees, threw a striking tableau into strong relief. Falcon was seated among the ferns, his long boots off, his head between his hands; in one of the boots the bushranger's arm was plunged to the elbow, presently to be withdrawn with a pad of crackling paper, folded like a cork sole. In his other hand was a similar packet, and he sat for a little with the two between his fingers.

"I'm going to stick to these two tots," said Power at length, "so you may as well tell me what they come to between them. Of course, I shall check your figures; but there's no hurry, we've not got to catch a train."

"Nor is it such a very large amount."

"How much?"

"Thirteen hundred altogether."

Falcon had not looked up; the outlaw's eyes were fixed upon him, and in their dark depths there danced a new light, a new humour, and an altogether new interest in the man with the head between his hands.

"And how came you to be riding like greased lightning with thirteen hundred pounds in your boots?"

"It wasn't my money," groaned the young man through his hands.

"Glad to hear it," chuckled Power. "I've no wish to ruin you, my son."

"But that's just what you are doing!" cried Falcon, looking up wildly. "It's not my money, but I'm responsible for it. It belongs to the National Bank of Australasia. I'm a clerk in the Euroa branch."

Power's eyes twinkled.

"That's all, sonny?"

"Why not?" asked Falcon, his wild eyes fixed suddenly on those of the bushranger. "What else do you think I am?"

179

"I don't hardly like to say," pretended Power, grinning outright. "I never did like hurtin' people's feelings; besides, I may be wrong."

"I'll soon tell you."

"Will you? Then I hope I'm right," exclaimed the bushranger, with encouraging emphasis; "for it did just slip across my mind — you'll forgive me if I'm wrong — that you was one of my own kidney after all!"

"Say it plainer."

"Well, then, I believe you've gone and done a bolt from that same bank with these same thirteen hundred and fifty pounds! In which case — "

"Well?" said Falcon, who had opened his lips to say something else.

"In which case," repeated Power gravely, "you shall have more than the odd fifty back again; for we shall be two of a trade; and there's honour among thieves — as long as I'm one of 'em."

"I'm glad to hear you say so," rejoined the bank clerk; "for I'm the other, and it's no use pretending I am not."

He was cool enough now, the younger rogue. He had made up his mind and accepted his fate, and it promised to be no such disastrous fate after all. Indeed, there were obvious advantages for the mere novitiate in crime, in a temporary alliance with a past master in the criminal arts. The clerk was (it has since appeared) a very clear-headed and calculating young man, who had yielded to no sudden temptation, but had put into unerring execution a plan laboriously laid in the coldest of cold blood. He had certainly lost that excellent head of his in the sudden presence of the one peril he had not foreseen, but he was now once more in full possession of his most distinctive faculties. He had therefore no hesitation in taking in his rather delicate hand the horny paw which was

180

now thrust over to him in tacit sign of felonious fellowship, nor did he scruple to tell the true story of his crime in compliance with the bushranger's request.

It was a sordid story, with no redeeming point. It was a story of manifold treachery, involving weeks of petty but consistent hypocrisy, and the final playing of a part which opened even the bold black eyes of Harry Power. As he said himself, it wasn't his way of doing things, nor was he sure that he would care to do that sort of thing in that sort of way.

"It's all a matter of taste," he conceded, "and you get the same for it when you're caught. Likely we shall meet in the hulks, one of these days, but I rather think I shall have the liveliest time to look back upon, always supposing I don't blow the brains out o' some spunky young chap like you, and swing according."

He sat looking critically at Falcon, while he puffed at a short b lack pipe which he lighted during the latter's narration.

"And you did show spunk with me," said Power, half to himself, "you loosed out upon me like a good 'un; and I'm not going to forget it. I know pluck when I see it, I'm like to know it. And there was no mistake about you there."

The compliment was lost upon the clerk. He had turned where he sat, and Power watching the sharp profile saw the visible eye protruding out like a bead. Next moment he had followed its direction and described the cause — a fitful glitter of accoutrements far away through the trees, clearly accompanied, in the sudden silence, by the faint but sharp ringing of well-shod hooves upon the flint-strewn track.

"Oho!" said Power; "so it's the traps, is it? Get you down into the gully; there, behind you, where the ferns are thickest. Down you go — right down — and down with your horse's head! Hang on to the reins like grim death! If his head don't

181

show, nothing else will; but I'll have to learn him different when he's mine!"

And at a whispered word his own worn veteran lay down like a dog, while the outlaw himself kept behind a tree, and the staccato tattoo of approaching hooves grew louder and more distinct.

"Can you see them yet?" whispered Falcon, who lay buried in bracken, his horse's head held close to his own by shortened rein and straining muscles

"I will in a minute. There's three or four on 'em. See here, son, if that moke of yours offers to neigh, you cuts its throat with this." And a villainous blade came swishing and glittering within Falcon's reach. "Stick him like a sheep," continued Power, "the moment he opens his teeth to it; but he won't do that if you hold on tight. Now, then, steady! There we are."

"How far off?"

"Not a couple of hundred yards; but they're sticking to the road all right."

"I hope they won't see my revolver!"

"I hope not. You were a fool to fling it. But I think it went well to one side, and you may trust a trooper not to see what isn't bang under his nose. Don't speak till I tell you."

The clerk obeyed, lying on his back, his biceps bulging, and the perspiration welling from a white face in imminent danger of being pawed beyond human semblance by his already restive horse. But the outlaw's horse lay like the clown's in a circus. And the outlaw himself did not practise what he preached, but apostrophised the white helmets and the bearded faces, as they went bobbing past upon the road below, in murmurs of half-affectionate abuse.

"You silly fools! You dear old fools! If only you knew who was lying in reach! That's right, look this way and welcome. A lot you can see when you're going full split! Oh, you fools; blind old, silly old, bloomin' old badgers! So long, then — so long — till our next merry meet."

Falcon turned on his elbow in the bracken.

"Is the coast clear yet?"

"I'd wait a bit."

The clerk counted a hundred slowly.

"Now?"

"I can hear 'em still. It's your moke I'm frightened of. But as you like; they must be nearly a mile away already."

When Falcon had finished stretching himself in the sun, he turned to the older criminal for the expert opinion and the skilled advice to which the situation clearly entitled him. Power had frustrated the final issue of his darling scheme; the least that he could do for a humble follower in his own footsteps, whom he had hindered instead of helping at the outset of his career, was to present him, from the wealth of his experience, with some new plan of escape in place of the one he had upset.

So hinted the clerk, and Power nodded with characteristic good humour. He seemed to realise his responsibility in the matter. The charge of unprofessional conduct, rather humorously insinuated by the other, was taken by Power in equally good heart. Yet he looked long and shrewdly at his man before replying.

"Native of this colony?" he inquired at length.

"No."

"New chum?"

"Not exactly. I came out from home the year before last. It was another bank bother. I was in one at home. They gave me so long to clear out or be run in."

The clerk was devoid of shame. The other looked him up and down before continuing.

"And how did you know the road so well?"

183

"I rode over it for my Christmas holiday."

"You had this in your mind since Christmas?"

"I had it in my mind since last July!"

Power maintained a longer silence than any hitherto. His dark eyes were half covered by reflective lids. His beard and moustache looked all one. Falcon grew restive under the prolonged scrutiny, he scarcely knew why.

"Well," said the bushranger at length, "I'm going to do with you what I've never done with any living man. I'm going to take you along with me for a bit. I'm going to show you where you can lie low for a month of Sundays if you like, with every trap in Victoria scouring the country for you. I've done it, so I ought to know. I'm going to let you do it, because I seem to owe you something, and you've got some spunk. But, my son, there's one thing I'm not going to do!"

Falcon waited to hear what.

"I'm not going to trust you. So I tell you straight. You'll go there blindfold, and you'll come back blindfold unless you can find your way out, and you're welcome to that if you can."

The bushranger paused again, took off his grey wideawake, and tapped his handsome head with firm forefinger.

"When there's a few hundreds on a man's head, on or off his shoulders," said he, grimly, "he don't put up for the Melbourne Club, nor yet pick his teeth on the steps of Scott's Hotel."

The rest of that day they journeyed together through the veriest wilderness, not trackless, indeed, but veined only here and there with the roughest bridle-path, and that not always visible to the clerk's eyes, which were left unbandaged after all. Time enough for that upon the morrow (said Power), for it would take them the best part of another day to reach his lair. Meanwhile they must camp somewhere for the night. And camp they did, in a rocky hollow, upon the jagged banks of a

184

tiny creek, that seemed to have lost its way amid the grim solitudes of the mountain forest.

It was a cheerless bivouac. The bushranger produced a box of sardines and a slab of very stale damper; these he divided with the clerk, but he would have no fire for fear of attracting the police; so the meal was eaten in darkness and washed down with very cold water from the creek. Now the month was March, when the sun is still its summer self, but the nights are the nights of incipient winter; and this was the first time the clerk had ever slept in the open; it was therefore not astonishing that he should begin shivering over his pipe as evening cooled and darkened into night. It so happened, however, that there had been a long silence between the pair, and that this broke it rather harshly; for it seems that the young man's bones were suddenly rattling in his skin.

"What's the matter?" asked Power, who was resting on one elbow, in such an attitude that he might have been watching the dim figure of his companion or might have been asleep.

"Oh, nothing," said the clerk, in a voice half startled, half relieved. "It's a bit chilly, that's all. But I thought you were asleep?"

"Maybe I was," said Power; "but, you see, I sleep with one eye open — and one ear, too. So you're cold, are you? That's soon mended. Lend us a hand."

He groped for Falcon's, found it in the darkness, and pulled himself to his feet.

"Well, your hand's not cold, anyhow," said he. "It's as hot as a coal. Have you got a bit of fever on you?"

"No," said he clerk, "I'm all right."

Yet his voice shook like his limbs.

"You may be," said Power, "and you may not. I've got a blanket for you, whether or no; so you may as well have the benefit of the doubt."

185

He detached a soft blue cylinder from his saddle which was slung over a low branch of the tree to which the horses stood tethered and at hand. Falcon, however, flatly refused to have it over him; he was not going to take the only blanket, and he said so with more heat than gratitude. But in mere will, like the majority of mankind, he was no match for Power, who was equally determined on the point.

"Why," cried he, "you may call this cold, but you wouldn't if you were used to camping out like me. I call it mild as milk; but then I'm as hard as a flint myself. The blanket's all I use in the depth of winter, and I wasn't even going to unroll it; but now I have you've got to curl up in it, whether you like it or not."

Nor was this all; for it seemed that the elder ruffian was prepared against emergencies with a flask, which he handed to Falcon, after tucking him up with his own overbearing hands. In this case, however, the clerk made no demur, but drank eagerly of the raw spirit before returning the flask without a word.

Not that Power resented the omission. The moon was rising through the trees, and the outlaw looked pityingly down upon the flushed but haggard face which its first rays touched. Clearly the clerk was ill; he seemed, nevertheless, to have fallen instantly asleep; and Power was quicker still to follow his example, with this difference, that the bushranger's nose at once announced his condition to all the sensual world within earshot of the cheerless camp beside the creek.

It was not this that awoke the clerk; he had never been asleep at all. His eyes had opened as soon as the bushranger's back was turned. He had lain for some minutes, glancing at the moon, still flushed and still haggard. Convinced at last by the time and timbre of the snores, he was now resting on one elbow, and his teeth showed white in the moonlight. They

186

were set. And the eyes were brilliants in a ghastly face. For in very truth the man was in a fever. But it was a fever of the mind and of the heart.

The scene is easily imagined. What passed in that fevered mind will never be known. Yet even at that one may give a fairly accurate guess.

Why should he be robbed in his turn? Why should he even share his ill-gotten gains with a greater villain than himself? Like many another, he had fallen a victim to the brutal rapacity of the notorious Power; unlike the rest, however, the clerk was not contented to remain victim to the chapter's end. It was his turn to get the upper hand, and get it he would. He was in any case a desperate man. He had flung his good name to the winds, he had no further right to his liberty, was he also to lose that for which he was risking and renouncing so much? Not if he could help it. But there was only one sure way of helping it. And it was the way that had whitened his face and brightened his eyes; it was the first conception of that way which had afflicted him with the ague of fearful temptation, with the fever of burning shame.

But now the raw spirit was at work in his brain, nerving him, hardening him, and he would not remember who it was to whom he owed his Dutch courage. Or if he remembered, he dismissed the consideration as a sentimental weakness. What was a notorious bushranger but a menace and a curse to society at large, to be shot down at sight like a mad dog? So Morgan had been shot at Macpherson's station — shot in the back — and yet the entire community had praised the deed. So Power

———

Falcon fell to trembling again, and loathed himself for his weakness. Perhaps, after all, he might give the fellow a chance, might call upon him to surrender, or at least wake him before he fired. It was not incumbent upon him — he would not admit that — but it might satisfy some sense of which even the clerk possessed a measure. Yes, he would have his chance; but what a chance it would be, the clerk knew in his heart; and, first of all, he must obtain possession of the rifle; for Power had not permitted him to recover his own firearm, and the little cartridges were rotting uselessly in his pocket. If only he could get possession of the rifle! Success or failure — spelling life or death — both hinged upon that!

During their ride through the bush Power had carried it slung across his broad shoulders; but had detached it before lying down, and now it lay loose at his side, with but the barrel, under the crook of his arm, gleaming steadily in the moonlight.

The clerk threw off the blanket which had been wrapped about him, and breathed more freely when rid of it. Then he rose to a sitting posture; then lunged softly forward upon his hands and knees.

He was actually kneeling over the prostrate man, who was snoring as loud as ever. One delicate hand was planted palm downwards upon the ground, between the sprawling legs; the other was creeping slowly towards the stock of the gleaming rifle. And blood was running down the clerk's chin, for his teeth were near meeting in his nether lip, to stop its trembling.

The rifle moved; the sleeper did not. In a single second it was withdrawn altogether, and — the tables were turned. Falcon knelt upright, trembling still, but yet able to cock the piece with the least possible noise. Now he was ready — now he would cry "Surrender!" in his turn. But he would not hesitate to fire. And then — then there would be an entirely new situation to face at his leisure. A few hundreds on his head! The ruffian had said so himself; they were his very own words. And what if he, Falcon, were to claim this blood-money — to profess that he had borrowed that of the bank merely as a bait? He would be forgiven, free, and yet have those hundreds to the good!

Meanwhile his mouth had grown very dry; he could not cry the one word needful without moistening it; and in the instant this took him, that happened which had been almost certain to happen from the first. A slight move on the sleeper's part — a sudden and relentless pull at the trigger — a wild cry waking the echoes of the silent bush — and the two men face to face in the moonlight. For the hammer had fallen with a harmless metallic click, and the cry had come from the clerk, who was kneeling still, but kneeling for mercy now.

Power was slow to speak. Slow also was his speech when it came.

"You blithering fool! So you thought I'd lie down with a loaded gun — and you! Didn't I warn you I wouldn't trust you? But I must have forgotten that myself to close an eye, with you handy. And to think — "

He sat silent, dumb with his contempt. Then a grim light broke upon his moonlit face.

"Why, I stuck you up with an empty gun, you silly! How do you like that? Make you feel better? But this one isn't empty," and he pulled out a full-sized Colt.

"That's it," cried the clerk, finding a high voice suddenly. "Shoot me — shoot me dead."

The bushranger shook his head.

"Not me, sonny! I don't waste powder and ball on such carrion as you, who'd shoot a man in his sleep for the blood-money on his head! No! there's nicer things reserved for such as you."

"What things?" shrieked the writhing wretch. "What? What?"

"You'll see, sonny! Oh, you'll see!"

But it was the police who saw best, for by a poetic irony (not unforeseen by Power) it was they who found their original quarry when returning on their tracks some hours later. They found him tied to a tree, close to the road where he had first been waylaid; with plenty of breath (and little else) in his body, but the circulation stopped in half his limbs; and over his head the following document, uncouthly printed with a burnt stick, and tied to the tree with strands of whipcord:

RECEIVED
From the national bank of
Australasia (Euroas B ranch)
per the undertied
(£1,350 0s. 0d)
Signed H. Power
His Mark for Life

And the mark, though fresh, inflamed, and greatly swollen, was a none the less plain round ring, burnt in the very middle of Falcon's forehead, apparently with a red-hot rifle barrel.

A Dog and his Day

Opinions differ as to the hour at which his day actually dawned; and the dog himself is the very worst authority on the subject. Some of us, however, fix the date by that issue of *The Times* which gave him a whole column of unqualified approval; while others put it a day or two later, when the *Pall Mall* made elaborate fun of him at equal length. It is said to have dawned upon Smith's officials at the bud of one week, and of the men of Mudie at the beginning of the next. It is certain that the novelist himself was longer in the dark than any other person concerned.

He never looked at a review; when at work, he was in the habit of leaving his very letters for days unopened. *The Times* cutting, which I took to him myself on the Sunday, he cast behind the grate unread; and would talk of nothing but the new work then on the anvil. About that, as usual, he was all enthusiasm. He hoped always to write a good book; he had long ago given up hoping to write a successful one. Nor was I at all sure that he had done so yet, though the departure had been for him a singularly new one. I was to be enlightened, however, in my turn, before the working week was many hours old.

On the Monday night, the Aaron Fullartons happened to be giving one of those celebrated receptions, which were unkindly said to owe their celebrity to Mrs Aaron Fullarton's connection with the half-penny evening press. It was not a very difficult matter to get an invitation. Previous publicity, of any sort, was the one credential required, and I was verbally invited (I should be ashamed to say on the strength of what) some fifteen seconds after my first introduction to Mrs Aaron Fullarton.

The civility was afterwards confirmed by card and repeated week after week with the kindliest iteration. Until the Monday in question, however, I had never been able to take advantage of it. But that night I went.

The Fullartons were then living in a very nice house in Sloane Street. The rooms were excellent for purposes of the sort, but it was the month of June, and terribly hot, for I found an even greater crowd than I had been led to expect. Also there were more really well-known persons. But one had no voice in the matter of one's companions — not if Mrs Aaron Fullarton knew it. Introductions were her strong point; I had heard it before, and now I proved it to my cost. She introduced without misery or remorse; you had no sooner escaped from one person, than you were led captive to another; or, if by luck you found common ground and made a temporary friend, you were walked off in ten minutes (I dare swear, by Mrs Fullarton's watch) to begin afresh on fresh material. Not that the material was always fresh; my hostess introduced me to one of my oldest friends among men, as well as to the lady who had originally presented me to herself. But there came a space in which she gave me peace, from *that* sort of trial, at all events.

It was before the buffet in the lower room. Something like a general conversation was going on; and I caught the name of Albert Hemming, and the title of his new book, *Faint Heart and Fair Lady*. To my delight, the book had been named to me once already during the evening and now I listened almost breathlessly for the general verdict of this highly literary assembly. What I heard was instructional, certainly; but it was not criticism, or even comment, on the book. It was partly wonder at the statements made that day by the young men in the libraries, and partly speculation as to whether, or how far, the demand was likely to continue. Figures were freely indulged in, and comparisons were made with the most successful efforts of some of those present. The point of view was the tradesman's with two or three exceptions. The exceptions wanted to know who Albert Hemming actually *was* — they seemed to know the name. Then one came up who described him to them as a literary hack and failure who drank like a fish and — but at that I could hold my tongue no longer. I spoke up, and to the point.

"Then you know Mr Hemming?" said my hostess in a new voice when I had done. "Take me upstairs, Mr Laurie. I want to speak to you."

"I have known him for years," said I, as we halted in the hall. My heart was still beating with indignation.

"Then bring him to my next Monday — or give me his address!"

"I doubt if he would come."

"Why not?" And Mrs Aaron Fullarton ran rapidly and proudly over the strongest names upon her list. "They have all been to one or other of my Mondays; why should Mr Hemming not come too? Does he think himself too good?"

"He would probably say he wasn't good enough," I rejoined. "He is not only a hermit, but just about the most shrinking soul alive."

"But only think what I could do for him," persisted my hostess, I must say with all kindliness. "You really might persuade him to come! Tell him I could give him paragraphs in twenty papers the next day, and interviews in at least half-a-dozen weeklies. Of course they would be judiciously spread about. And I'm always so careful; I wouldn't say a thing he could mind, or create the least suspicion of log-rolling or anything horrid! Do say you will do what you can!"

It was so kindly meant, in spite of the main chance underlying all — the *quid pro quo* so transparently genuine — that I divulged Hemming's address and said I would do what I

193

could. I felt it would be little enough; but I promised, and was thereupon introduced to a young literary woman who talked about her "art" and her aspirations until I longed to sink through the floor. I tried her on Hemming's novel. It was no use. She never read any fiction except her own; it interfaced with her "art". She desired to influence, not to be influenced — and the rest. After that I was on my way to the door, but fell in with young Wynne, the short-haired poet, who saluted me with a wink.

"What are you doing here?" he asked. "I didn't know this sort of show was in your line."

"No more did I," was my reply. "I'm just off."

"Oh, you mustn't go yet," said Wynne; "why, the fun's only just beginning. The Countess has only just come."

"Good heavens!" said I.

"Not an English Countess, you understand. Can't quite place the nationality."

"How do you spell it?"

"Spell that Countess? With inverted commas, if you ask me!" chuckled young Wynne. "But come and see her for yourself; then I'll tell you all about her. I've found out a thing or two since she was here last week."

But even as we turned my companion gripped my arm; and there was our beaming hostess entering the room with a woman whom to see once was never to forget. She was a tall, upstanding woman, not a little stout, but straight as a steeple, and very handsomely dressed in grey satin that gleamed like a knife where the light caught it. This was relieved with touches of a pink so delicate that I can only liken it to the lady's own complexion. She had the face of seventeen, with uncommonly large blue eyes, and golden hair; but what struck me most was the glow of youthful health upon the plump, smooth cheeks. It was not artificial, yet with so matronly a figure there was something unlovely in such loveliness. One thing I thought: she wore too many diamonds, and there was that in her smile which made me set her down at sight as innately vulgar and untrue. Yet there was also that which made me doubt whether she had been so always; in a word, I was half fascinated, wholly repelled. I looked for Wynne, but he had left my side, and was making his way to this woman's. Five minutes later I was introduced to her myself.

Her voice was as young and soft as her face; she spoke admirable English, with a foreign accent of the slightest; but we had not exchanged many words before I saw it was the accent, and not the English, which she had acquired. She herself confirmed my impression. Strictly speaking, she was the Contessa Cordella — her husband had been a Portuguese — but she was herself of English birth. All this, once more, she told me in the manner of a school-girl of seventeen; only now I could see for myself the tiny wrinkles round her eyes.

"Are you an author, too — or an artist — or both?" she asked me with her curious smile; and when I told her that my claim to either title was so slender as to be almost baseless, she shook her yellow curls. "You are too modest," said she. "You are all authors here, or artists, or something. Not an actor, however."

"Indeed!" said I. "How do you know?"

"Because you cannot conceal your feelings."

"And what feelings have I betrayed?"

"Your disgust at being introduced to me!"

"Oh, I am shy," I said. "I suspect I always look like that."

"You are clever," she replied — "and I love clever men. That's why I come here. Tell me — do you happen to know Mr Hemming?"

We had found places on a settee, but I nearly started to my feet with joy.

195

"Albert Hemming?"

"Yes, of course — the novelist."

"I know him well," said I. "Have you also been reading his work, and do you like it?"

"I have, and I like it more than I can say. It makes me long to meet the man."

"You are not likely to do that. He never goes anywhere. I only wish he would. But he is the best fellow and the sweetest character in all London, and I am downright grateful to you for speaking about him as you have done!"

Indeed, I had warmed to the woman in a minute; her blue eyes were so full and liquid with enthusiasm; and then she had read the book before aspiring to know the man.

"It is going to be a great success," she said, softly. "Everybody is talking about it — here and all over. Tell me about Mr Hemming. He is married, of course? Where does he live?"

"He lives in a flat not a mile from this house, but he has never married."

"Then he lives alone?"

"No; a niece of his keeps home for him."

"A niece! But surely you know —"

She stopped, but not in time.

"You know him yourself," I said. "Why question me?"

"I have met him — more years ago than I care to count," said the lady, as she used her fan. "He has probably forgotten me, but you may take him every friendly congratulation on his splendid book —"

"From the Countess Cordella?" I asked.

"Yes; and you may give *me* his address.

"He never goes out —"

"Then I shall write to his publishers!"

I gave the address, and, bowing to the Contessa I went in search of young Wynne. During the foregoing conversation I had more than once encountered his eyes bent upon us with a frown. But now that I wanted him he was not to be found. And want him I did, with all my heart, and for an obvious reason.

Wynne knew something about this Contessa Cordella. The Countess knew something about my dear old Hemming. And *I* knew enough of Hemming's life to wish to know more of this woman.

But Wynne was gone; when I ascertained the fact, I also said goodbye to my hostess, and how-do-you-do and goodbye to her husband, whom I did not remember to have seen before; and Mrs Aaron Fullarton loaded me with a final charge with which to bring down the author of *Faint Heart and Fair Lady*.

"Tell him it wouldn't stop at paragraphs," she said. "I hear his book is going into a second and third thousand simultaneously and at once. If it reaches its tens of thousands I should be very glad to propose an illustrated interview to the Editor of the *Piccadilly*; and I would do it myself. That would mean photographs of the drawing-room and study at Cheyne Mansions, of Mr Hemming himself at all ages, and a specimen of the manuscript of his great success. So do bring him next week and let us talk it over!"

I said, falsely, that I would do my best — if I saw him during the week — which was doubtful. Twenty minutes later, I was climbing the stone staircase on which the jets of gas had long been turned down to tiny stars. But a higher light shone as usual through the grand glass of Hemming's door.

Hemming opened the door in list slippers and no collar and tie. By his lighted eye and the pen in his hand I perceived him to be hard and happily at work. A warning finger further informed me that Irralie Villiers had gone to bed; indeed, it was after twelve; yet I felt disappointed. I had known the pair sit up together until the smallest hour.

"Now you may talk — for a moment," said Hemming, as he pushed me into his little den and pointed to the wet manuscript on the desk. "Nobody can hear us in here."

"But you're busy. I won't say a word till you're done. May I take off my coat and smoke?"

"You may take off your skin so long as you don't bleed on the floor," returned Hemming, whose jokes were frequently of a gruesome character. "Here's my pouch. Go and help yourself while I finish my chapter — only go quietly. It won't take me ten minutes."

And with that he was down at his desk, and writing as fluently as though I had never come in; nor did he look up or speak for an hour and a quarter by my watch. His pen was going freely all the time. I sat still and watched him from the easy chair.

The room was a den indeed, and that of one dead to appearances, yet redeemed from outer savagery by the close companionship of some guardian angel, not his wife. Irralie was an angel with clipped wings and limited control; no wife would have brooked the squalid chaos of Hemming's study. Books were its most respectable feature; but they lay in a dusty disorder on the crowded shelves, like a scratch garrison at drill. Irralie might not touch the books, nor the proofs, which hung over the backs of chairs, or dangled from the walls caught in clips. Yet my eyes found her handiwork on every side. The single picture which possessed a frame, and was not an illustration to one of Hemming's stories — torn out and tacked up anywhere — the one deliberate thing of beauty in the room, had been a birthday present from his niece. There were flowers

198

on the desk, half-hidden by the accumulation of newly-crossed sermon paper, and insulted by the close society of reeking pipes and miniature ash-pits. I knew whose hand had placed them there. Even the writing-lamp by which he worked was the gift of the girl.

How he wrote and wrote! My chair was to his left, and a little behind him. I could see chiefly the curve of his broad, round, threadbare shoulders, and the dome of his rough, grizzled head as he huddled over his task. Puffs of smoke swirled about it at first, like mist about a mountain; but as he lost himself in his task, his pipe went out, and I heard him set it down. The dip and scurry of his pen was almost continuous, and when I changed my position I could seldom see more of his face than a wedge of whisker and half a lens of his spectacles. But once he leant back in his chair, and stared at the lamp's green shade, feeling a phrase; and then I had a better view. He had the fine, bulging forehead of the imagining man, and a profile which glasses and a beard could not spoil. To me it seemed all in a tremulous glow from his fancy's flight. As he stared at the lamp, his beard broke across in a smile; he stabbed his pen into the ink, and went on.

He was happy then — happy in what he was doing, not in anything done. He little dreamed of his success. Yet that success seemed assured. I felt reluctant to tell him of it, and knew not why. A doubt stole over me — I despised my heart for admitting it — an ignoble doubt as to whether we should see the same sweet soul on the top of the wave that we had loved and honoured in the trough of repeated failures. Success is an ordeal no easier to bear than defeat: the fires of success burn at a whiter heat, wherefrom only the truly great come forth unhurt. I knew of no alloy in Hemming. I loved him, as Irralie loved him, for a thousand virtues which we found in him, still more for the thousand littlenesses we said we had but he had not. Even Irralie had a temper, and some vanity; but he had neither. So I, his inferior, had mean forebodings on this the eve of his triumph, who deserved to triumph if one man did in the world.

So my thoughts ran as I sat in his chair, watching him; and I was ashamed of them. I may say, however, that they were not consciously connected with the woman of the golden hair. That garish vision was slow to follow me into Hemming's den.

At last I heard him give a deep sigh, and throw down his pen. I rose and looked over his shoulder. The half-filled sheet which finished the chapter was numbered ninety-four.

"Nearly a hundred pages already!" I cried; "and you only began the other day. What form you are in! Read me some of it."

Hemming shook his head.

"Six chapters, my boy, and I don't say I haven't seen worse. Still it isn't fit for you to hear. There are similes to import etc and sentences to spruce up. When it's finished, though, and I've sorted it up and down, it ought at all events to be the best of my things. *Faint Heart* won't be in it — I will say that. I wonder if it'll do anything?"

He had slipped the warm manuscript into a drawer, which he locked mechanically. He sat a moment without speaking.

"*Faint Heart* is doing something," said I, meaningfully. And I watched him intently; but his face did not change.

"Very kind of you to say so," he remarked, as he pushed back his chair. "Sit still while I get you what your offensive pride wouldn't let you get for yourself." He was back in a moment with spirits and a syphon. But I was not sitting. I stood with my back against the cast-iron over-mantle, and I eyed him severely.

"What do you suppose brought me here at this time of night?"

"Been to a party: wanted to take the taste away. No wonder!"

"Been to a party and heard everybody talking about *Faint Heart* — that's more the size of it! I tell you it's the success of the hour. Congratulations!"

Hemming only thrust a tumbler into the hand I had held out for one of his. "Say when," said he; "and don't talk straw or I shall take it from you."

"Confound you," I said, "can't you see I'm in earnest? I've been to a sort of literary-artistic show — such a crew of painty and inky sinners as never was seen in one room before! Long hair — pale faces — and the price of words on every lip. And on every other lip — *Faint Heart and Fair Lady*! You may shake your head, you mountain of mock-modesty, but it's the sacred truth. My hostess clamoured for your address. She wants you to go next week and be advised and asked how it's done. I said you wouldn't; nor will you."

"Who is the lady?" enquired Hemming, puffing his pipe; and I told him what little I knew of her. I may have added a little more that I had only heard — and perhaps it was not added kindly. Hemming at once took characteristic action, and I found him high and dry on the side of the woman whom I had maligned more by unconscious importation than by deliberate word.

"She must have an uncommonly kind heart," he said, "and if I had a dress-suit I'd feel inclined to go. But my last went mouldy from disuse; and, besides, I don't believe she *did* say all that; in fact I hardly believe a word you say!"

Thus it became necessary to repeat the speeches of Mrs Fullarton word for word; and when he had heard them, Hemming was more than ever convinced of that lady's disinterested goodness of heart. He was a man who could see no guile. He had lived by himself so long, or, rather, with so sweet a child for his sole companion, that he looked himself upon the world through a child's trusting eyes. And here was one secret of his past unsuccess. The psychological novel had for years seduced him, and his psychology was an innocent as his own heart. But *Faint Heart and Fair Lady* was a fresh departure — pure romance and a contribution to the romantic revival most happily timed.

He was wilfully, insolently slow to believe any news. He had never taken his romance very seriously, nor would he its success. Besides, the whole thing might be a flash in the pan; yet the very way in which he said this, revealed his humorous indifference as but a cloak to his emotions. Then success was sweet to him as to others. When was it not to the healthy human tooth? And Hemming was beyond all things heathy. Three was striking in another room, and morning light beginning to wrestle with the lamp, for all the curtains, when he bared me his soul a little lower yet.

"I wish it was the other three," he said: "I should like to tell Irralie. If there's any truth in what you say, and there really is a success in the air, she and I are to set out and see the world before we go any farther. That's an old promise — a grand tour of our own!"

It was my turn to fear. To change the subject I told him of the woman with the yellow hair, and gave him her message with a very keen eye upon his face. He looked hugely mystified and droll; pulled his beard and shook his head.

"Not golden," he said; "I don't recollect ever getting mixed up in anything of that colour." His manner changed. He became curiously grave. A drawer was unlocked, there was a feeling among relics, and then Hemming thrust under my nose a wisp of brown hair lying in a crumpled piece of paper. "You don't call that golden, do you?"

"No," I returned. "Whose is it?" For it was rather a dark brown, and I thought at once of Irralie Bouverie.

"My only love's," declared Hemming, with affected melodrama. But he put the hair very carefully away, and, as he did so, broke into poetry, which he could recite very well, being a poet at heart. This was the poem:—

"My only love is always near,
In country or in town
I see her twinkling feet, I hear
The whisper of her gown.

She foots it ever fair and young,
Her locks are tied in haste.
And one is o'er her shoulder flung,
And hangs below her waist.

And, yet her voice is in my dreams,
To witch me more and more —
That wooing voice. Ah me! It seems
Less near me than of yore.

She ran before me in the meads;
And down the world-worn track.
She leads me still, but while she leads
She never gazes back.

Lightly I sped when hope was high
And youth beguiled the chase;
I follow, follow still, but I
Shall never see her face. "

As I say, he repeated poetry with the feeling of a poet. But this little lyric moved him to a tenderness of voice and eye, which one who heard and saw can never hope to describe, for which reason I transcribe the well-known lines at length. It was as though they came from his very heart, as the words of another do more often than any our own hearts can frame. There was a silence in the little room, and the edges of the curtains took a hue more distinctly gray. At length in my ignorance I asked who the verses were by.

"A poet's work — or I don't know one when I see him. Never say die while you've a shot in your locker or a locker on your shelf!"

So he was laughing it off, for it was not in the man to give a loose run to sentiment. His humour kept ever from him his blackest moods, like lightning on a summer's night. But at this moment we heard the London sparrows in the gardens behind the flats. Hemming drew the curtains, and threw the sash up higher. Then he stood as I shall never forget him, with his burly figure against the grey sky; and quoted more poetry in his rich, sad voice.

> "Ah, sad and sweet, as in dark summer dawns
> The earliest pipe of half-awaken'd birds
> To dying ears, when unto dying eyes
> The casement slowly grows a glimmering square;
> So sad, so strange, the days that are no more."

Again we were silent; and this time comment would have been profane. But now the mournfulness of the man communicated itself to my spirit; and I rose and went, taking with me his sadness but not his serenity. For both had been conspicuous in his character ever since I had known him. And it was now my uneasy lot to wonder, if success removed the sadness, whether it would leave the serenity unruffled as heretofore.

Of one thing, however, I was thankful as I walked to my rooms in the cool June morning, through the desolate white streets. I was thankful it was not a wisp of golden hair that Hemming treasured under lock and key.

My morning paper was the next to sing the praises of Albert Hemming and his new novel. The issue was printing in the same small hours I spent with Hemming in his little den. I read it in my bed that forenoon, and the first thing I saw (in large capitals on the second page) was a speaking headline:

THE ROMANCE OF THE YEAR

That was enough for me. There could be — there was — but one new book to answer to that name. I put down the paper and lit my pipe. Then I took it up again, and was not disappointed. Nothing could have been stronger, certainly; nothing kindlier or more enthusiastic; and if the praise was almost oppressive, I am bound to say it did not oppress me. I got to my work, and stuck to it against the grain until well on in the afternoon. Then I made myself decent, put the newspaper in my pocket, and proceeded hot-foot to Cheyne Mansions.

Hemming was out. I held my breath; but Irralie was in. In a moment I was awaiting her in the little drawing-room which reflected her personality as the study reflected Hemming. It seemed full of sunshine all day long, and of summer flowers all the year round. The flowers were not my imagination. The girl had a very little money of her own, and this was how she spent it.

205

Irralie herself was a slip of a child still in her teens; but a great heart beat in that slim figure; the small, proud head was older than its years and her face I thought the most beautiful in all the world. She came in immediately with her fine frank smile and her fast and heart handshake.

"Oh, Mr Laurie, I am glad you've come! You are the very person I wanted to see."

"Nothing wrong, I hope?" said I. "Where's the author?"

"I don't know where he is. There *is* something wrong, but it isn't that; I can't think what it can be — when everything ought to be so right! Oh, isn't it splendid about *Fair Heart*? And it was you who brought him first wind of it; but of course it would be you!"

She looked at me so gratefully that I felt ashamed. "You ought to pitch into me for keeping him up so late," I said. "Do tell me what has happened."

Irralie shook her head.

"Yes, that was very bad of you; but you literary men are hopeless in that respect. He never went to bed at all. He was waiting for me when I got up, and he brought me in here, and told me all that you had told him. Naturally he was in splendid spirits; he said, if it was true, that he would take me to Paris and Vienna, and Switzerland and Italy. Only think of it! There was no end to his plans; still he seemed to think you might be mistaken, and that though *Faint Heart* might do better than his other books, he greatly doubted whether it would be a real success after all. You know what he is when he is making plans: up one moment and down the next: so when he went down I just opened my bureau and got out the press-cuttings. I subscribed unbeknownst for the notices of *Faint Heart*; I felt they would be good; but I determined not to show him one of them until plenty had come in, and there could be no doubt about the matter. So I showed them to him this morning. I made him read them. And when he had finished, he put on that queer look of his, with his eyebrows up and his eyes down; but *he* wasn't down any more. Indeed, we were never so happy in our lives, for the reviews have been magnificent, as you know; and he seemed pleased with me; and I felt so proud of him. But just then — "

"One moment," said I. "Here's the best of the lot, which you won't have seen yet, owing to your uncle's abominable conservatism." And I handed her my morning paper.

Irralie looked at the article, then read it through; and when she looked at me her eyes were wet.

"Yes, it is indeed the best," said she. "Oh, to think that anything should have happened now! Let me finish what I was saying. Just then the letters came, and the first he opened was better than all the reviews put together. It was from the publishers, confirming your report about the second and third editions of *Faint Heart*, and offering to buy his new book unread! The bid is for serial rights and everything!" concluded Irralie, forgetting her bad news in her good; and now her eyes only sparkled.

"Then there was some other letter?" said I.

"There were two other letters. The first was merely a card from your friend Mrs Aaron Fullarton; he showed it to me; but he never let me see the other. Yet I saw more than he suspected. I saw his white face and fumbling fingers. And I saw the coronet on the envelope."

A coronet! I could have laughed aloud; but, indeed, to us who loved him it was no laughing matter. I looked upon Irralie and her sweet anxiety, and I thought it better not to mention the Countess Cordella to her. Indeed, it was obviously none of my business — the woman was an old flame of Hemming's, that was Hemming's affair. I still hoped it was not so, but if it was it had nothing to do with me. Nor could any power make him poor; but the future was another matter, and my sole feeling was that our friend should not fly twice at that same yellow flame.

"Where has he gone, Miss Villiers?"

"I have not the least idea."

"When did he go out?"

"About twelve o'clock; and now it's four!"

"Forgive the questions. Any trouble in this flat is a trouble under my hat — which wasn't mean to rhyme. You said your uncle hardly spoke to you after he read that letter with the coronet. Was he writing his book?"

"No — letters. He came to me for two stamps."

"Ah! One for our universal hostess; the other — "

"Hark!" said Irralie. It was a key in the lock; in a moment Hemming was in the room.

He made a quaint figure in the pretty, sunlit drawing-room. He wore the same old clothes as overnight, but they looked still older by light of day. The only additions were a whitish muffler and a villainous old hat crammed upon the back of the head. But the expression beneath its brim, and indeed the man's whole carriage, pleased me better. For his eye had the strong, level light of the soul that has fought and conquered; and as a further token of his triumph he carried himself for once erect, with lifted head and shoulders square. He told us what he had been doing. He had spent several pennies on the river-stream boats; had been down as far as Greenwich, where he asked us to believe that he had treated himself like a king; and had left behind him the cobwebs of late hours and hard work. For the first time in all the years that I had known him, he further confessed to feeling healthily sleepy and tired; also (despite his boating) to an immediate desire for tea.

But all was not well with him yet. I knew it when Irralie was out of the room and he made no reference to the woman of

208

whose existence I had myself informed him but a few hours before: of the letter which he had been warned by me to expect. And more than ever I knew it by the little charmless topics he *did* touch upon; but most of all by his extraordinary lack of interest in the best review he had ever had in his life. The critic's enthusiasm did not strike a spark from Hemming; he was still too nervous, too restless, and too *distrait* After tea nothing would serve him but that he and I should go out together for a stroll; and when I hesitated (being extremely happy where I was), he found a pretext, changed his mind about the stroll, and from the open window called a hansom.

"Your tailors!" said he. "You've got to take me there. I want that dress-suit!"

"Have you accepted the invitation?"

"No; but I've written the lady an amiable letter; and I may go if she's good enough to leave it open."

"*If!*" said I.

"Then I asked if I might take Irralie; and if I may, my dear, you shall have a new frock out of my second edition, and I will change my waiter's livery against the third. Faith, I wonder how I'll take the tape-measure again after all these years! Guess I'll lash out like a mule: shouldn't wonder if they have to survey me by theodolite!"

But I had no heart for his jests: the girl had her arms round his neck, but it was not of him that I was jealous. Irralie was already entranced at the double prospect of her new garment and of Mrs Aaron Fullarton's "reception". Heaven knows there had been little enough of that sort of pleasure in her young life! I knew it too: yet the thought of our wild-flower in that hot-house filled my fine-made soul with unutterable indignation. I shook her hand without kindness, and went out ashamed.

209

Hemming in the cab was as silent as I. When he did speak, however, he startled me.

"Do you think," he said, "that your titled friend will be at Mrs Fullarton's next week?"

"I have no doubt of it," said I, "in fact, she told me she would."

And that was all; but I was not deceived in his tone; and in the small, bevelled mirror on his side, I watched the struggle in his face. When we alighted, and had paid the cabman, Hemming stood before my tailor's door, shamefaced, and would not let me pass.

"I have thought better of it," he said. "I *should* lash out; besides, it might injure your credit. Let us go for that stroll instead."

It was now between five and six of a flawless summer's afternoon. The week before had been Ascot week; and my dear companion did, perhaps, render us a conspicuous couple, as we turned our faces to the westering sun. I know at least that I thought so, with many little thoughts, as I sought and dreaded a possible acquaintance under each immediate silk-hat. And I know too I loathed myself for those base terrors; and that, notwithstanding them, the man at my side was something dearer to me than all but one only in the world.

We went to the Park. Grosvenor Gate was our point of penetration, and we walked past the statue of Achilles through the thick of the throng towards Knightsbridge. Hemming's comments were amusing. But I was not amused. I had to take off my hat once or twice; and there was Hemming's arm through mine; and yet I loved him. A third time it happened, and my arm swung free. The little Victoria passed on, with the hot sun flaming in the woman's hair. Hemming, breathing hard, stood still. His face also was on fire. But the sun upon his spectacles hid his eyes.

"Turn back," he said, thickly.

There were no more words between us. What was there that one could say? And Hemming was always ahead, treading on fairy skirts, elbowing fine frock-coats; and so we found ourselves once more at Grosvenor Gate.

"What now?" I asked.

"I've changed my mind."

"Again?"

"Yes, again. You needn't come with me, Laurie. I remember the shop quite well."

That night I hardly slept. I was uneasy about Hemming and the woman with the yellow hair, as well as on another score as little my concern. The introduction of a girl like Irralie to a circle like the Aaron Fullartons' was a subject on which I took myself very seriously indeed. I idealised the girl, was prejudiced against the circle, and had yet to attain my twenty-fifth year. I fancy no more need be said; save that the worst part of the matter was a haunting feeling that I had already offended Irralie over the head of it. At least I had looked on her ecstasy with a stony eye. I had said good-bye to her in a stony voice.

Little things became big things in the night. It was no little thing, however, that finally robbed me of this particular night's rest. I will neither mince my meaning nor enlarge upon it: I had long been in love with Irralie Villiers, and now I felt unable to keep it to myself another day. Yet how was I to speak? Hemming whom I went to see was always with us at the flat; besides, my desserts were very small. Then I feared to lose my darling friend — and that was a sickening fear. But further I will not follow the familiar coil of intertwining hopes and fears. I determined in the end to dare my fate. And I chose the literary method. Sunrise saw me shivering in my dressing-gown over the warmest letter I ever wrote; and afternoon found me with that letter in my pocket instead of in the post.

I could not face the long hours of suspense; and ultimately I hit upon a compromise. I would go the flat with the letter in my pocket. I might not need it after all; but (like a swimming-belt) it would give me confidence; and if my tongue finally refused to come to the rescue of my heart, well, at the worst I could deliver my letter with better effect than the postman. So I went.

Hemming was in. Irralie was out. I confess my first feeling was one of ridiculous relief; even the apprehension, with which the subject of Hemming filled me, was a new apprehension, and, to a man asking all in the place, almost a boon. My old friend was in fact very wretchedly depressed. I found him idle in his armchair, and in such a condition that my own anxiety could not live in his presence.

"Well, Laurie?" he said. And his voice was as kind as ever; but he neither rose nor returned my grip.

"Well, sir!" said I. "And what's the trouble?"

"I'm stuck. I can't go on."

"Since when?"

"Oh, since you were here the other night. I can't start the next chapter. I've tried again and again, but I've given up trying for the day."

"You've been doing too much; don't think about it, and it's bound to come."

"Ah, but I can't help thinking!"

He ran five fingers through his grizzled hair.

"About that?" said I.

"About what?" he asked sharply.

"Your work."

212

"Yes — about my work," he said; and his tone forbade further intrusion. Nor did I regard what he said — so shortly, for him — as the mere blind it might appear. I knew, or thought I knew, the length and breadth of his extremity. Of one thing, however, I was sure: that in such a life the refinement of every misery must be the consequent inability to work. To see him in trouble, and denied that anodyne, without being able or allowed to say a word to comfort him, was enough, indeed, to distract me from my own hopeless case; yet it was Hemming who brought me back to it, and that very suddenly, after an interval of silent smoking.

"I was thinking of Irralie," he said.

"Irralie?" cried I.

"Yes. I am troubled about the child. I am troubled altogether."

"Why about Irralie?" I asked him, tentatively. He was a man with whom it was possible to go too far. He was also some twenty years older than I.

"Why about Irralie? I will tell you. That child is all the world to me; but she's not a child any more, and it's only just come home to me. She's lived with me so long! Ever since her father brought her home from India, and left her with me when he exchanged regiments for the express purpose of getting killed in Zululand; and he had his wish. Ever since then I've had her, and a dull life it must have been for a young girl: little schooling, less pleasure, and hardly a friend outside my doors. Perhaps it's been a little brighter for her since we came to live in town. We've explored London, the two of us, pretty thoroughly at odd times; but all the time I've treated her as a child. Yesterday, only yesterday, I saw she wasn't one any more. I hardly know what it was: something in her excitement about next Monday and her new frock, I suppose it must have been, that opened my eyes. Anyway they're wide enough open

213

now. She's out about that frock at this moment. She talks of nothing but next Monday night. And now I don't want to take her at all."

"You don't?" I cried, joyfully. "Then why not back out of the whole thing? I assure you it's not the house — "

Hemming shook his head. I stopped, reproved.

"I don't care what it is, I'm not going to disappoint her now; I'd rather cut my hand off. Still I fear it. I'm sorry I promised. Laurie, if I was to lose her it would be the death of me! If anybody was to take her away from me, I mean!"

He leant forward, with all the vague suffering in his face suddenly and sharply refined. My heart raced. I seemed to hear it beat against the unread love-letter in my jacket pocket. I nodded, for I could not speak.

"If I was to lose her," he continued, "I don't think I could bear my life. Life isn't worth it if you've nobody to love and live for. Work isn't worth it if you've nobody to love and work for. And now that there seems a chance of my being more successful, I could make it up to her in pleasure, and travel, and entertainment; oh, if anybody took her now, it would be cruel! Laurie, you must help me. You are the best friend we have. You must help me to keep her by hook and crook! At present you mayn't know what I mean; one day — "

I jumped up. I was about to tell him that I knew quite well what he meant; but at that moment we heard the bell; and his face that had been so worried became transfigured with joy.

"There she is!" he cried. "Let her in, like a good fellow."

I went to do so, but even through the opaque glass of the front-door I could see in a moment that it was not Irralie. I returned and told Hemming. To my astonishment, he bounded to his feet, but went no further than the study door.

214

"Not at home!" I heard him tell the servant in an agitated whisper. "We are all out, and nobody is to be admitted on any pretext whatsoever!"

The front-door and that of the study, though at right-angles to each other, were close together; and now they both stood open, and I recognised the voice on the landing, but that was all. But I saw Hemming trembling as he stood with his back to me, an unseen listener to the words I could not catch. Then the front-door shut; the servant handed Hemming the cards, and he faced me, tearing them to little pieces with a nervous spasm such as I had never seen in him before.

And not a word to me; it seemed never to occur to him that I, too, knew Cordella's voice when I heard it; evidently, on the other hand, where the Contessa was concerned my sympathy was not invited. My curiosity, however, was now excited as it had never been heretofore. Why should he wish to meet the woman one day and not the next — in a stranger's house and not in his own flat? Was he (as I had before suspected) inspired as much with dread as with desire? And what had he to dread; and why should he tear up the woman's cards, as if they were herself, and hide them so carefully away in his waste-paper basket? This done, he turned to me with a pale face, certainly, and resumed the interrupted topic with a vigour which seemed to me to belong to those emotions which I was not allowed to share.

"Promise me that in case of need you'll help me to keep Irralie — to myself!"

I promised, thinking less of him than I had ever thought before.

"Swear it!"

To humour him, I swore it too.

"Thank you," said Hemming, taking my hand. "Now I'm going to tell you something you won't be sorry to hear. I'm

215

not going to take her to that evening after all. Will you help me to get out of it?"

"With all my heart. I never did think it the sort of thing — "

He cut me short. His mood had changed. He was now sufficiently alert in mood and bearing. And through his spectacles there shone a candid light that heralded an admission before it was made.

"That's not the point. The point is — and you know it as well as I do — that I am going to Mrs Fullarton's to meet, chiefly out of curiosity, an old friend of nearly twenty years' standing. But I have my own reasons for not wanting Irralie to make her acquaintance; and that's the whole truth. Think no more about it, like a good fellow, but put your mind to helping me out of this little scrape with Irralie. I have a notion the opera would be a pretty efficient substitute; what do you think? And, if we decide on that, do you mind buying me a couple of stalls when you're up tomorrow?"

I accepted the commission, of course, though I could not but mention what I believed to be the price of opera-stalls at the height of the season. That did not matter. The more the better. Irralie must have first-rate compensation for her disappointment; besides, there was a good time coming, from all accounts. And with her name upon his lips, Hemming heard the girl's step through his study wall (which abutted on the stairs), and rose to go and meet her.

"And you stay where you are," said he. "She and I must have this out together."

I stayed where I was for a quarter of an hour, but to me the time was like an age. I wanted to see my darling, and yet I wanted to see her not. For how could we meet so often and still be only friends? Bitter as I felt against Hemming, however, when I took from my pocket the letter which must now be destroyed, I could still see a case for his selfish fears.

They were not entirely selfish. Irralie was after all very young, if not too young to know her mind; whatever she might say, it would be a sin to make her say it now. And I — if I loved her — I could surely wait; only one has not learned to wait with a very good grace at five-and-twenty.

Heaven knows if I had made too sure of my answer; in that case, at all events, I was well and promptly punished. For, when they summoned me, I went into the drawing-room thinking how terrible a fate it would be to remain mere friends with Irralie Villiers. And, even as I took her hand, I knew that we were considerably less than friends already. She would not look at me; would scarce favour me with replies, much less a remark; and told me what she thought of me, in her own honest fashion, the first moment we were left together.

"What have I done?" I was fool enough to ask.

"Done?" said Irralie, with a high proud look that made me love her more than ever. "Am I to condescend to tell you what you've done?"

"If you please," said I humbly.

"As if I didn't know you had put my uncle against the Fullartons' in order to rob me of one of the greatest treats I could possibly have had!"

"I!"

"Yes, you. I saw how you looked when he spoke of taking me yesterday. It is very kind of you, I must say, to suggest where I should or should not be taken!"

"But I have said nothing to influence Mr Hemming one way or the other. He is not acting from anything *I* have told him," I said, warmly, for Irralie could make scientific use of her tongue, as I now discovered to my cost.

My protestations, however, were of no avail. "I know what you have said," she rejoined, "as well as if I'd been in the room at the time."

"Did your uncle tell you?"

"No — but I know."

"Then I shall not attempt to disabuse you. You are doing me a complete injustice; but perhaps it is as well!"

And so I left her, to construe my words as she would or could, and, as she chose, to regret or glory in her own upon reflection. The fighting light was still in her eyes. The fighting colour was yet upon her cheeks — I told a lie to Hemming, and I went straight home to burn the letter in which it was written that I would live or die for Irralie.

The tickets for the opera I forwarded by post next day.

The Cricket on the Green

Some seasons ago, ere the world went astray —
    When summers were sometimes serene —
A match which the natives recount to this day
    Was played upon Whizzingham Green.

'Twas the ultimate round — called the Final 't'would seem
    For the Inter- Parochial Cup;
And the sides were the glorious Whizzingham team
    And the village of Hurry-cum-Up.

Quite early, came bustling and hastening in
    Spectators from near and from far:
They all took a fence until play should begin,
    And studied the *Whizzingham Star*.

The way that they'd measured and marked out each crease,
    Quite agreed with the canons of cricket,
But — as someone observed on surveying the piece —
    One couldn't say much for the wicket.

"What with buttercups, daisies, and cowslips," said he,
    "Not to mention these hillocks and lumps,
When I stand up to bowl I declare I can't see
    The top of the opposite stumps!"

This critical youth would have spoken untruth
    To a Judge in a Court of Assize;
So no one rejoined (since the charges were coined) —
    Save by furtively dropping their eyes.

The toss it was won by the Whizzingham crew:
    The visitors went out to field.
Mid cheers the first pair strutted forth into view
    The Whizzingham willows to wield.

The first was the Squire, Sir Tommy de Vere,
    Who by Yorkers was never enticed.
His bat (like his name) had a handle, 'twas clear,
    And that handle (like Tommy) was spliced.

My lady sat anxiously watching her lord —
    He would start with a sixer, no doubt.
But, the first shot, his mainmast went clear by the board,
    And the Whizzingham captain was out!

And — alas for the shocking example thus set! —
    The batsman who followed his chief,
Though known as a punishing bat (at the net),
    Came promptly and sadly to grief.

Two for ducks! — the whole village was piping its eye —
    Was there nobody good for a stand? —
When their languishing spirits were lifted on high
    By the strains of the Local Brass Band.

And at last, when the bowler came down with a wide,
    And scoring in triumph began,
Though the notch was a gift from the opposite side
    Still the multitude roared to a man!

Then Potts broke his duck and seemed in for a score,
    For he knocked both the bowlers about;

Till charging his Comrade while running a four,
    He was forced to retire — "run out".

But Twist, the professional, came on the scene
    And landed the bowling all over —
Though plenty of trefoil besprinkled the Green,
    Yet the fieldsmen were securely in clover! —

So that long-stop, accurst with a terrible thirst,
    (Being much put about by-the-*bye*),
Had signalled like mad to the Publican's Cad,
    And was cooling his throat on the sly.

When a ball, swift and true, hit him full on the shoe,
    Recalling his wandering wits: —
Though he thwarted the run, it was flukily done,
    And the tumbler was smashed into bits.

The whole of the innings we may not review,
    But at last, to the joy of each scout,
(If it seems paradoxical, still it is true)
    The last of the in-side was *out*.

Twist carried his bat, and he bowed with doffed hat,
    While the crowd yelled in praise of his stickin'
Making flattering guess at his future success —
    But the Whizzingham pro. was no chicken!

Now their aggregate score (I've not mentioned before)
Was precisely one-hundred-and-seven;
Which to beat — 'gainst the cream of the Whizzingham team —
Was a hard nut for *any* eleven.

At three when the heat of both teams had been drowned,
    (Bottled beer and superlative "cup"),
The bell rang out loudly for clearing the ground
    For the innings of Hurry-cum-Up.

Now the speedy and summary way that the fate
    Of the earlier batsmen was sealed,
Wasn't stranger — allow me at once, please, to state —
    Than the pranks of the men in the field.

The total was twenty, with five wickets down —
    Sir Tommy de Vere was elated,
When in came young Pulham of slogging renown,
    And Sir Thomas's bowling was slated.

Though the ball was pitched straight he would mow it quite
                       square
    (To which hits none that day hold a candle),
But alas! — though his bat fairly hummed through the air,
    Yet he kept a loose hold on the handle.

So that luckless long-leg — which had wintered in France,
    And was therefore no very great shakes —
When the bat was sent flying by horrid mischance,
    Was restored pretty quickly to flakes.

Well, nothing was scored though the fieldsman was floored,
    And they carried him off on a shutter:
But Pulham made runs — what with twos, threes and ones
    And the aid of a scandalous "butter": —

Long-on and long-off they both rush for a "skier",
    Each showing the best of his paces;

They see not the pit — from their heels spurts the mire —
    They roll in each other's embraces!

The others yelled "Shame!" at the top of their bent
    (It was strictly a genuine charge!)
But the fallen used words which by common consent
    Are assigned to the crew of a barge.

Then the fieldsmen went terribly down on their luck:
    Mid-wickets, especially slack,
Threw so wildly that all with amazement were struck —
    But the umpire was struck in the back!

And the latter, not slow to resent such a blow,
    Went after the ball at a hobble
And hurled it like lead straight at mid-wicket's head
    Which nearly led up to a squabble.

The while there's young Pulham increasing his score —
    You'll study his style, let me beg? —
And watch how he drives the half-volleys for four,
    And places the short ones to leg!

But this leg-pulling tendency threatened to lead
    To an Inquest and Criminal Law,
When the Umpire, — who gathered no sinecure's mead —
    Saved his head by the veriest straw!

Cover point was not destined to shine in the field:
    For a ball bounding over the slopes
Went clean through his legs — which he actively wheeled
    And dashed to save tour to the ropes;

But he tripped and fell sprawling on top of the ball —
      And he called his mates "venomous varmints",
And other bad names which I need not recall,
      When they lifted him off by his garments.

Well, Pulham had his wicket upset
      By one of the baronet's twisters;
And nine wickets fallen and thirty to get,
      Foreshadowed defeat for the vis'tors.

The people resolved that the game was a farce
      Which would quickly be closed by the curtain;
(And drinks were diluted and customers sparse) —
      But cricket was *always* uncertain!

For the very last pair, with resolute glare,
      Set their teeth, and with confidence played
(And the Publican's Cad was exceedingly glad
      Since it brought him revival of trade.)

Sing, Muse, of the stand of that valorous pair —
      Of the way that they mastered the bowling!
Sing, Muse, the excitement that buzzed in the air,
      And the plaudits like thunder-peals rolling!

For Oh! With their voices at fort — is — si — mo
      The Hurry-cum-Uppers they hollared! —
But the Whizzingham wheeze was *piano*, you know,
      For their bowling was Collar'd and Collar'd!

Sir Thomas, in changing the bowling, incurred
      His comrades' outspoken detractions;

But though this was productive of singular words,
      It produced still more singular "actions".

(Ye bowlers who'd have your antagonists vext
      By premature doubts and alarms,
Just study the style of the figure annexed
      And copy this comrade in *arms*!)

But just as the plot was approaching its thickest.
      Mid the hush of solicitous crowds,
Young Timms — who was scoring a long way the quickest —
      Hit a ball out of sight in the clouds!

It soared (so they say) many miles into space,
      To the sun crying "hail fellow — *well* — met!"
Then dropped right in front of the gate-keeper's face
      Bang on top of Z70's helmet

Z70 gazed at the shot-spattered hat;
      Z70 swore he'd not stand it;
Then he rushed with a yell at that violent "bat",
      Nor paused for a magistrate's mandate!

Now the match was a tie; and when clear through the din
      Young Timms heard that arrogant shout —
Says he "Though you're bent upon running me *in*,
      I'm bent upon running 'em *out*!"

Then he lifted big bat — though a "Cobbett", I wiz,
      It was sprung ever after this date! —
And the way that the match was played out after this,
      Village history does not relate.

225

Some say that all parties adjourned to the tent
  And joined in a general tea-fight;
While others (who claim to have seen the event)
  Contend that the fight was a *free*-fight.

And as for Z70 — prostrate and stunned,
  They bore him away on a litter:
But Timms was imprisoned; and afterwards shunned
  As a rather too dangerous hitter!

FINIS

NOTES

The Stroke of Five   Published in *Belgravia* in Nov. 1887.

The Cooeying Woman   Published in *The Queensland Figaro*, 8 Oct. 1887, and probably elsewhere as well.

Cabin-Companions   Published here for the first time — the manuscript is in the Cadbury Research Library of the University of Birmingham University, catalogued as item MS 127/A/2/1/4.   It was written when Hornung was living at 49a Waldegrave Park Road, Richmond, in the late 1880s, after returning home from Australia.   Taking this information into account with the large, rather clumsy handwriting in which it is penned (very different from his later style), suggests that it was written no later than 1887 or 1888.   The notion of a son taking revenge on the absconding partner of his father, bankrupted as a result of his partner's treachery, is one that would have been particularly dear to Hornung's heart at this time.

The Stockman's Cheque   Published in *The Speaker*, 27 July 1895.

Long Jake's Trip Home   Published in *Chambers's Journal* in two parts, June 1889.

Miss Teague's Behaviour   Published in *The Chicago Herald* on 25 July 1891, and probably elsewhere as well.   [The editor must plead guilty to having replaced the rather lame rhetorical question with which this story originally ended ("Why are women so staunch?") by one more in harmony with the text which had preceded it.]

The Romance of Sergeant Clancy   Published in *The Idler*, April 1892.

The Crimean Shirt   Published in UK newspapers in May 1898 and in *The Star* (Australian newspaper) in Oct. 1898, but subtitled 'A Christmas story' which suggests that it had probably been published five or six years earlier in the December issue of a magazine.

The Burrawurra Brand   Published in *The Idler*, Nov. 1893.

The Man that shot Macturk   Published in *Pall Mall Magazine*, Sept. 1895.

A Lochinvar of the Old Man Plain   Published in *The Graphic*, summer issue of 1899.

The Best of the Bushrangers   Published in *Manchester Weekly Times*, 16 Nov. 1900 — but probably written a year or two earlier.   An unusual tale, in that Henry Johnston, or Henry Power (1819-91), was a genuine bushranger.   One wonders whether the author had originally intended it to be a 'Stingaree' story.   (Another story about Power, which harks back — in advance! — to this one, had been published in *The Sphere* on 27 Jan. 1900.)

A Dog and his Day   Published here for the first time — the manuscript is in the Cadbury Research Library of the University of Birmingham University, catalogued as item MS 127/A/2/1/3.   The author's address is written in the top left-had corner of the first page of the manuscript — "14 Rossetti Mansions, Chelsea" — where he lived from 1893 until 1897. The two extracts of poetry quoted by Hemming come, respectively, from 'The Unrealised Ideal' by Frederick Locker-Lampson and 'Tears, Idle Tears' by Tennyson.

The Cricket on the Green   This is the text of a small *jeu d'esprit* production, running to 32 pages, which Hornung produced in collaboration with a solicitor-friend called Richard Edward Wethey (1861-1935): Hornung wrote the verse and Wethey supplied the illustrations. It was published in 1895 by Jordison & Co Ltd, a firm based primarily in Middlesbrough (Hornung's birthplace) but with an office at Ludgate Circus, in central London.